M000192273

DAILY DISCIPLINES

90 DAYS OF PERSONAL GROWTH

SKIP ROSS

with contributing authors
Mike Cooke
and
Melody Farrell

THIS BOOK IS PUBLISHED BY LOST POET PRESS

All rights reserved, including the right to
reproduce this book or portions of this book
in any form whatsoever.

Text copyright © 2015 by Lost Poet Press and Skip Ross
Jacket art by Rob Stainback copyright © 2015 by Lost Poet Press

Copyright (c) 2015 by Lost Poet Press.
Published by Network TwentyOne International, U.S.A., 2016.
All rights reserved.

Published in the United States by Lost Poet Press
First paperback edition.

No part of this publication may be reproduced, stored in a retrieval system, or transmitted
in any form or by any means, electronic, mechanical, photocopying, recording, or
otherwise, without written permission from the publisher.

www.skipross.com
www.thrivestudy.com
www.circleacamp.com
www.lostpoetpress.com

ISBN 978-0-9914489-6-8
ISBN 978-0-9914489-8-2 (ebook)

Library of Congress Control Number:
2015949063

For worldwide distribution
Printed in the U.S.A.

Lost Poet Press first edition paperback printing, October 2015

CONTENTS

8	**FOREWORD** by Melody Farrell
10	**FOREWORD** by Mike Cooke
12	**INTRODUCTION** by Skip Ross

14	**Day 1:** Process of Change
16	**Day 2:** Positive Affirmation
18	**Day 3:** The Dark Room
20	**Day 4:** React or Respond
22	**Day 5:** Seeing Through New Eyes
24	**Day 6:** What Does it Take?
26	**Day 7:** Dreams and Goals #1: *What kind of dream?*
28	**Day 8:** Dreams and Goals #2: *Healthy discontent*
30	**Day 9:** Dreams and Goals #3: *Fearing our dreams*
32	**Day 10:** Dreams and Goals #4: *Facing the critics*
34	**Day 11:** Dreams and Goals #5: *Write down your goals*
36	**Day 12:** Dreams and Goals #6: *Paying the price*
38	**Day 13:** Dreams and Goals #7: *Checkpoints*
40	**Day 14:** Do It Now
42	**Day 15:** Gratefulness
44	**Day 16:** Comparison
46	**Day 17:** Choices #1: *Small choices*
48	**Day 18:** Choices #2: *Balance is a choice*
50	**Day 19:** Choices #3: *Responsibility is a choice*
52	**Day 20:** Choices #4: *Happiness is a choice*
54	**Day 21:** Choices #5: *Forgiveness is a choice*
56	**Day 22:** Choices #6: *Love is a choice*
58	**Day 23:** A Healthy Diet
60	**Day 24:** Flexibility
62	**Day 25:** Perseverance
64	**Day 26:** Procrastination #1: *Introduction*
66	**Day 27:** Procrastination #2: *What is procrastination?*
68	**Day 28:** Procrastination #3: *Consequences of procrastination*
70	**Day 29:** Procrastination #4: *Recognizing procrastination*
72	**Day 30:** Procrastination #5: *Avoiding procrastination*
74	**Day 31:** Humility
76	**Day 32:** Delegation
78	**Day 33:** What Am I Great At: Part one
80	**Day 34:** What Am I Great At: Part two
82	**Day 35:** Falling Short
84	**Day 36:** Why Daily?
86	**Day 37:** Teachability
88	**Day 38:** Tough Questions
90	**Day 39:** Accountability
92	**Day 40:** Personal Integrity
94	**Day 41:** Look for the Good
96	**Day 42:** Urgency
98	**Day 43:** An Honest Look
100	**Day 44:** Affirmations Revisited
102	**Day 45:** The Critic Within
104	**Day 46:** Superhighways to the Land of Your Nightmares #1
106	**Day 47:** Superhighways to the Land of Your Nightmares #2
108	**Day 48:** Superhighways to the Land of Your Nightmares #3
110	**Day 49:** Superhighways to the Land of Your Nightmares #4

CONTENTS
CONTINUED

112   **Day 50:** Superhighways to the Land of Your Nightmares #5

114   **Day 51:** Superhighways to the Land of Your Nightmares #6

116   **Day 52:** Comparison Revisited

118   **Day 53:** Competition

120   **Day 54:** Values

122   **Day 55:** Is it worth it? *#1: Time allotments*

124   **Day 56:** Is it worth it? *#2: Risk relationship Testing*

126   **Day 57:** Is it worth it? *#3: Rearrange your personal preferences and priorities*

128   **Day 58:** Is it worth it? *#4: Radicalize your habit patterns*

130   **Day 59:** Be Your Own Best Friend

132   **Day 60:** Why Did I Do That?

134   **Day 61:** Patience

136   **Day 62:** Momentum

138   **Day 63:** Significance

142   **Day 64:** Roadblocks to Significance: *Introduction*

144   **Day 65:** Roadblocks to Significance *#1: Lack of personal integrity*

146   **Day 66:** Roadblocks to Significance *#2: Competitive comparison*

148   **Day 67:** Roadblocks to Significance *#3: Loose talk*

150   **Day 68:** Roadblocks to Significance *#4: Negative Belief*

152   **Day 69:** Roadblocks to Significance *#5: Nonproductive relationships*

154   **Day 70:** Roadblocks to Significance *#6: Taking your eyes off the road*

156   **Day 71:** Roadblocks to Significance *#7: Eliminating the photo spots*

158   **Day 72:** Roadblocks to Significance *#8: Accelerating in neutral*

160   **Day 73:** Roadblocks to Significance *#9: Looking for the shortcuts*

162   **Day 74:** Roadblocks to Significance *#10: Lack of self-discipline*

164   **Day 75:** Roadblocks to Significance *#11: The new driver syndrome*

166   **Day 76:** Roadblocks to Significance *#12: Leaving your hand on the scale*

168   **Day 77:** Refuse Inferiority

170   **Day 78:** Conflict

172   **Day 79:** Priorities #1

174   **Day 80:** Priorities #2

176   **Day 81:** Priorities #3

178   **Day 82:** Loyalty

180   **Day 83:** Lead by Example

182   **Day 84:** Observation

184   **Day 85:** The Comfort Zone *#1: Introduction*

186   **Day 86:** The Comfort Zone *#2: Where does it come from?*

188   **Day 87:** The Comfort Zone *#3: A shielded safety*

190   **Day 88:** The Comfort Zone *#4: Group dynamics*

192   **Day 89:** Parameters

194   **Day 90:** It Takes a Lifetime

196   **CONCLUSION**

198   **CIRCLE A RANCH AND THRIVE**

200   **WORKS CITED**

202   **BIOS**

FOREWORDS
BY THE CONTRIBUTING AUTHORS

FOREWORD BY **MELODY FARRELL**

What an incredible journey this project has been for me!

This book was initially meant to be a collection of transcripts from the series of *Daily Disciplines* podcasts that Skip, my dad, released a few years ago. It was both a pleasure and a challenge to go back through the transcripts and try to distill 90 days worth of written lessons and thoughts to share, but the results have turned out to be something truly compelling. At the same time that we were going through the old podcasts, Dad was creating some new, amazing material (see the sections in this book about Roadblocks to Significance and Superhighways to the Land of Your Nightmares). Also, we received some requests from Leadership Team members of Circle A to cover some of Dad's most beloved staff training week teachings, like priorities, flexibility, observation, loyalty, and so on.

What has emerged from all the efforts and ideas is a book that I am extremely proud of. Truly, I feel like this book is a concentrated summary of all the wisdom that my dad has gleaned from his many years of teaching and ministry and business development and everything else. I have been profoundly influenced by investing the time to go over these principles for the last few months. There is no doubt in my mind that I will be reading this book myself, again and again, in the years to come.

When I read the foreword on the following pages written by Mike Cooke, it filled my heart up with an overflowing hope that the effort put into these pages by my dad, Mike, our team, and myself will be *more than worth it*. His story is just one of the thousands of life stories that I have personally seen influenced because of my dad and the legacy he is leaving. I am honored to play a small role in passing this wisdom down, and the best part is that I too get to change for the better.

I am so grateful for the opportunity to have worked on this book, and I am particularly excited to share it with you. My hope and prayer is that your story would be influenced towards a path of significance in life, and that together we can all become the people that we are created to be.

FOREWORD BY **MIKE COOKE**

First, I have a confession. When the *Daily Disciplines* podcasts first aired, I listened to two. Only two. Somehow the busyness of life came along and while I knew they were out there and I had access, I didn't listen to them. Fast forward to summer 2014. My life had gone through massive changes. My young son had passed away at the start of the year. This was devastating. I went through a depression and anger and thought I was better, so I went back to work. I lasted about a month and I couldn't function at work, so I went on leave again. I was being medicated, and on some level it helped. However in the big picture I was getting worse in a hurry. On the surface things may have looked okay, but within I was extremely angry. This continued to get worse until it finally boiled over. The slightest things would set me off. My marriage was falling apart. My wife stopped communicating with me out of fear of igniting my anger.

At about this time I got the opportunity to start working on *Daily Disciplines*. I started to read through the transcripts, correcting some simple things and putting them into order. As I read, I found wisdom for all the struggles I'd been going through. I was reading from my greatest mentor and a man who has been a father to me. He was sharing his struggles: how he battled them and what brought about victory. He talked about how his thinking had been changed. I related so deeply to Skip. Despite the fact that these original transcripts had been recorded years earlier, it felt to me as though he had written them to me just recently for all that I was going through.

Before the death of my son, I had attempted to live my life with Skip's *Dynamic Living* seminar as a blueprint. I had learned many additional lessons from Skip because of my closeness to the family over the years, and I had always intended to become the person I was truly created to be. But life had done its worst to destroy me, and coming back to these principles and thought processes was an enlightening and healing experience that I couldn't have anticipated. As I devoured each lesson and page, I saw clearly the errors I had made and the things I was doing wrong on a daily basis. I was convicted, in the gentlest of ways, that I was making poor choices and not taking responsibility for my life.

I started to implement things to help me change on a daily basis. I was reminded that massive change, which is what I realized I needed, starts with a single step. And for massive change to happen, new habits had to be established. I needed *Daily Disciplines*. I started reading scripture every day. Reading the daily lesson became a habit and it led me to add other things in from *Dynamic Living* as well. I am now writing and reading affirmations daily. I read my goals every morning every night. I am working on a description of the person I want to become. The ideas in this book are life changing, when we choose to apply them. My wife Maria has reminded me of this countless times as she has been pursuing her own healing and redefining after our son's death. She serves as an amazing example to me of how life can truly be beautiful and redeemable after even the worst of circumstances, and I am so grateful for the way she has led us both towards healing and growth and positive change.

Big goals are accomplished through the achievement of smaller goals. There is a quote that has been above the mirror in the bathroom of the boys' bunkhouse at Circle A Ranch that says, "The key to your success is hidden in your daily routine". As I started to make these changes, this quote sort of rocked me. Knowing the principles is great, and it's a big part of the battle. However, I understand now more than ever that daily implementation is the crucial factor that truly determines success.

In essence, that's why this book was developed. It looks at issues we face and battle on a daily basis and gives us an opportunity to take steps to overcome them.

INTRODUCTION

WHY DAILY DISCIPLINES?

Congratulations on your decision to engage with some positive, thought-provoking ideas! Whether you are a long-time student of personal development material, or whether this is your first exposure to any sort of this type of teaching, this book is for you. *Daily Disciplines* is a simple way to commit to a habit pattern of personal growth. A few minutes a day will make a world of difference in the way that you approach projects, business, relationships, parenting, studying, and life.

Here's the good news: ideas change the way we think.

And when we change the way we think, *everything* changes. My hope is that as we commit to 90 days of deliberate reading and thought for just a few moments together, we'll engage some ideas that will change our thinking for the better.

I have learned that by surrounding myself with thinkers and ideas that challenge and inspire me, I can continually work towards the betterment of myself and the clarification of my purpose in life. I deliberately look for the people in my life who will aid in this process by helping me to engage in healthy, meaningful, focused thinking—and my hope is that this little book will be a tool to help you do just that.

There is something singularly effective about a deliberate, daily commitment to a process. Sure, you could read this material all in one sitting and perhaps your mind and heart would retain much of it and you would be able to apply it to your life with great speed and enthusiasm. In my experience, however, there is a deeper meaning found when these principles are encountered over a period of time. The habit of engaging this type of thinking is perhaps even more important than any specific teaching itself – because when the *habit* is formed, we have a whole lifetime of growth and change that is open for the discovering.

So … let's begin!

- Skip Ross

DAY ONE
PROCESS OF CHANGE

In the process of change, we oftentimes run into difficulties. We want the change, we want to engage with the new ways of thinking and we want to apply that thinking in a way that takes us down a healthy and fulfilling path. But life tends to constantly get in the way with discouragements and distractions, and though we desire the change, we can so easily get derailed from any movement towards it. We fail to see the possibilities of positive growth and change that are inherent in any difficulty.

I've managed to find a few ways to combat those hard times, and today I'd like to tell you about one of those methods. I have—still in my possession after all these years—a tattered, dog-eared, well-worn notebook that describes the kind of person I want to be. I wrote this description many years ago, and I still revisit it often. I am still committed to the process of becoming that person.

Most people in the world never take the time to decide what kind of person they want to be. That's unfortunate. If you don't have a target to move towards in the area of personal growth, it becomes that much harder to find the motivation to move at all.

I want to encourage you today to begin to develop this idea. Find a notebook, or a journal, or even just a few scraps of paper, and start to describe the person you want to be. Perhaps an app on your smart phone can hold the powerful words that you will write—it doesn't matter where you do it, it only matters that you do.

If you have already started something like this, get out that description and revisit it. Maybe rewrite it in the context of where you are today. If you aren't sure what you are doing or what to write, don't worry—just begin the process. Remember, you have a whole lifetime to tweak and discover and learn and grow. Today, it's just about beginning that process of change and refusing to stay in a place of paralysis.

As we move along in our 90 days together, there will be a short exercise at the end of each day. My suggestion would be for you to get a journal to use to write a couple brief thoughts at the end of each reading. When you have concluded this book, you should have a wealth of statements and ideas from which to begin forming a more complete picture of the person you are created to be.

Exercise: *Write 10 words here that describe the person you want to be. These adjectives will help you begin the longer process of a detailed description.*

DAY TWO
POSITIVE AFFIRMATION

I want to encourage you today to begin the process of writing and reading positive affirmations – and then to use it for the rest of your life. Many people who understand this technique tend to use it only for brief periods of time, starting and stopping on the whims of distraction and disruption.

I encourage you to make it a regular process—decide the things that are important in your life and affirm them. You can do this in every area of life where you desire to see positive change—work, school, health, family—the list goes on.

Here are a few examples to get your mind thinking about what you might want to affirm.

> I am patient with those who see things differently than I do.
> I radiate strength of purpose to everyone I meet.
> I am honest with others and I am honest with myself.
> I maintain a positive mental attitude at all times.
> I speak well of everyone.
> I am decisive and I am confident of the decisions I make.

Those are just a few examples from my personal book of affirmations – and there are many more where that came from. I didn't come up with them all at once, but there was a process of deciding that I wanted these things to be true about me, and then there was the action step of putting them to paper.

As you prepare to write your own, let me give you a few suggestions. These are statements that are made about *you*. They are not statements designed to control the reaction or behavior of other people. Of course it would be a desirable thing to be able to know that people would be affected by what we say and affirm about them. And indeed, words of encouragement that we *speak to* others benefit both them and us. However, this is about affirmations. The reality is that we can make affirmations for ourselves … and that's about it. The good news is that when you make affirmations about yourself, you begin to change. And when you begin to change, you create an environment that other people will respond to. In *that* sense, we can help our relationships with other people and how they treat us.

I hope you also noticed that all of these sample statements were written in the present, positive tense—that means they should be written as if they are happening right now. The statement should not be written as though it is something you want to become some time in the future, but rather something that you currently *are*. It's okay if they are not currently true about you – the point is that you want to write them as if they are true today. I would have to admit that some of these things that I wrote about myself were not true at all on the day I first wrote them. They were still yet in my future, and I wanted them to be true, but I needed to speak about them as though they were *already true*.

Exercise: *Write one affirmation about yourself here. Write it in the present, positive tense.*

DAY THREE
THE DARK ROOM

Not too long ago I happened upon a fortune cookie that contained this statement: "Fear is the dark room where negatives are developed".

Before the vast majority of pictures were taken on phones and stored digitally, we took pictures with a camera and the image was burned onto film. Then the film was taken to a room and placed in a chemical solution to print the images onto paper. This process had to be done in a dark room because *the images would be lost if the film were exposed to light.*

Let's think about this in terms of life. Our mind is constantly receiving the input from all the experiences of our lives, and the fact is that we are going to have negative experiences. If we allow these negative experiences into the dark room of fear, then they develop into pictures that we accept into our visual narrative of reality. We allow ourselves to become more and more fearful of all the terrible things that may happen to us.

Let me illustrate this with a practical example. When I was young, I had an intense fear of the dark. It started one night when my mother put me to bed, tucked me in, and turned out the lights. I looked up through the blinds of my window and saw a pair of eyes looking back at me. I was so afraid that I tried to scream but nothing came out. Finally I was able to call for help, but by the time my father ran outside, the man had escaped – all that was left were his footprints in the flowerbed.

For some time after this, I had a fear of the dark, a fear that continued to grow based on other experiences that I allowed to affect me. My mind had taken a picture of the frightening experience and allowed that picture to develop into a debilitating fear that if I went into a dark room, something bad would happen.

Negative experiences *will* happen. That's life. We are left with the choice of what to do with them. If we allow our thought process to focus on the negative experiences in our lives, our minds will turn into a dark room where the sketchy thoughts will be developed into full-blown experiences. These experiences will build a fear in us that will cripple us from becoming all that we are created to be. However, if we purposefully focus our thinking on the good, positive, creative, and inspiring experiences of life, our minds become filled with light. And in the light … the negatives cannot be developed. It's just not possible.

Exercise: *Write down 5 positive things that you can focus your thoughts on today.*

DAY FOUR |
REACT OR RESPOND? |

One of the statements that I wrote many years ago in my journal of the person I am becoming says this: "My actions are based on what I know I should be doing and not on my emotions. My emotions are ever changing."

This is an important point to recognize. We cannot take control of our lives and live the kind of lives we are created to live if we do not realize that our decisions and reactions cannot be based on our emotions. We must take charge of those emotions and understand that they are neither the healthiest nor the wisest determiners of our actions.

You and I both know how frequently this happens. What seems to be a great day is all of a sudden dashed to the rocks by an unkind word, an unfortunate occurrence that is out of our control, or by something that happens to a friend or family member. Suddenly, we go from happy and upbeat to defeated and miserable. Our emotions are always in flux and they change frequently on the basis of the circumstances in which we find ourselves.

So here's a question I've learned to ask myself when a difficult situation arises and I am tempted to make a decision led by my emotions: am I reacting based on the way that I feel, or am I responding based on the truth?

When we view our actions through this lens, we can sometimes see ourselves choosing to react. For example: we get too busy, so we skip the gym. We have a difficult phone conversation at work, so we talk unkindly to our spouse because we need to vent our pent-up anger. We convince ourselves that we deserve to keep our bad attitude because of our bad circumstances. We find out that our AC needs repair, so we cancel a business meeting out of frustration and weariness.

Sound familiar? These are all *reactions*. They are understandable in the moment, perhaps sometimes even excusable ... but do they lead us to becoming all we are created to be? Perhaps not. The better way to live life, then, is to realize that our emotions will change, but the decisions that we make need to be based more upon what we know to be the right thing rather than on the emotion of the moment.

This is easier said than done, of course. Reacting is always more instinctive than responding. However, as we train our minds and hearts to choose response instead of reaction, my belief is that soon our responses will come more naturally and innately based on truth and reason instead of emotion.

Exercise: *What is one positive decision you can make today that you will refuse to allow any emotion to alter?*

DAY FIVE |
SEEING THROUGH NEW EYES |

For the most part, our growth comes step-by-step, ounce-by-ounce. We don't always see our progress from day to day and it's only after a period of time invested in pursuing growth that we can look back and see the advancement that we've made. But sometimes we move to a new level of understanding all at once. It's one of those, "Eureka, I found it" type of experiences, the "aha" moment where everything we have been working so hard to understand suddenly comes into focus.

As I have moved along in my years, my vision has begun getting dimmer and dimmer, and I have needed stronger and stronger reading glasses. The time came a couple of years ago where I needed to have some surgery on my eyes so that they could function at a higher capacity. The doctors went into my eyes, took out the old, dim lenses and put in brand new ones.

And I have to tell you … it was an "aha" experience all right! Suddenly I could see things both up close and far away. I could recognize people at church from a distance. Everything had come into such focus, a clarity that I didn't even fully know I was missing.

The same thing can happen with our thought processes and our personal development. Although perhaps it can't be planned and prepared for as my surgery was, it can certainly be expected. As we continue to pursue our dreams and the betterment of ourselves and our lives, we will run into these "aha" moments from time to time.

We will wonder how we have read the same quote so many times before and never truly understood it. Or we will suddenly gain a perspective on a relationship or a fear or a trial that completely solves a problem we have been wrestling with for years.

Here's what I'm discovering about it: it's all about a process of maturity and growth. As we commit to the process, even here, by reading *Daily Disciplines* each and every day, we will experience the "aha" moments more and more. Just like kids grow daily, but sometimes have massive growth spurts that seem to come out of nowhere, we will have growth spurts in our personal development.

I'm believing with you today that you will receive some new lenses soon so that you can see your life with new eyes, eyes that are matured and focused with the lenses of commitment, passion, and purpose.

Exercise: *What is an area of your life where you have committed to a process of growth, but you are ready to experience an "aha" moment?*

DAY SIX
WHAT DOES IT TAKE?

There are differences in life between those who achieve greatness and those who simply do not achieve anything that they feel is worthwhile with their lives. Oftentimes we can get caught in a web of our own excuses, reasoning that our success is perhaps more difficult or even unattainable because we do not have the conditions or experiences required for success.

We sometimes believe that a healthy family background and upbringing help to bring about success. While that may be a beneficial factor, the truth remains that huge numbers of successful people come from broken and dysfunctional families. In fact, you could probably make a list of many people you know, or know of, that have risen above their difficult past and been successful.

Is it wealth, then? Do financial resources equate to a higher degree of success? Again, there are many who come from poor and meager beginnings and still become successful.

Is it opportunity? Some say that those who excel in life just got the breaks. They were in the right place at the right time. Opportunity smacked them in the face. You know what I believe? I believe that *all of us* are in the right place at the right time. The real question is: do we observe the right time? Do we find the courage to take action? Do we believe that we "deserve" the right time and the right place?

Is it moral excellence? There are some who believe that a life lived according to a high standard of morality is the key. I wish that was the real reason why people excel, but we all know seemingly successful people whose lives are not based on any sense of morality at all. Though I certainly believe that there are moral principles that will greatly influence a person to be both successful and significant, I have also observed that many can achieve all sorts of things without the commitment to those principles.

Does success have to do with an absence of hardships? I don't believe so. In fact, if anything, it might have more to do with a presence of hardships. We have all heard story after story of people who have only made something great of their lives after being faced with tremendous pain. Then again, not every story is filled with life-shattering hardship either.

What is it that causes people to excel?

I think that perhaps there is more power in asking this question than there is in answering it just yet. And so, I'll leave it there for today.

Exercise: *What do you believe is necessary to move past mediocrity? Are there any characteristics of peak performers that are universal?*

DAY SEVEN
DREAMS AND GOALS

#1: WHAT **KIND** OF DREAM?

"Always remember there are only two kinds of people in this world—the realists and the dreamers. The realists know where they're going. The dreamers have already been there." – Robert Orben[1]

This quote reminds me of a story I heard about a group that was on tour at Disney World several years ago. They were going through Epcot. Someone said to the tour guide, "Isn't it a shame that Walt Disney never got to see his dream?"

The tour guide turned and with great surprise said, "What do you mean? It all existed in Walt's mind before it could ever exist here in reality."

This is true and certainly inspires us to dream. However, it seems to me that the dreamer also needs a touch of reality as he moves along the pathway of life. He must realize that though it is good to dream, it will remain only a dream unless he recognizes and persists through the things that get in the way of that dream becoming reality.

So let's think for a moment: *What is it that gets between me and my dream, my goal, my vision for my future?*

One thing we need to recognize is that there is a major difference between "daydreaming" and the process of focusing on a real dream. A real dream, with hope of becoming reality – one that we can get our thoughts and feelings around – is a completely different type of thought process. I like to call this type of dream a daring dream.

The daring dream is focused on the actions, thoughts, goals, and disciplines it will take as part of the path to reach the dream. The mental energy involved with a daring dream is an energy of determination, assessment, planning, vision, follow-through, and passion.

In contrast, the daydream relies on luck or happenstance as the only way to get to the destination. If you have a daydream, there is nothing particularly wrong with that. It's fun to just kind of "blue sky" and daydream from time to time. Sometimes this can even help us see a bigger vision. But the mental energy involved only in wishing or imagining without a commitment to action will never allow those dreams to become realities in our lives.

Today, let's begin to think about the things in our lives that get between us and our dream. Are we dreaming the right kind of dream? Are we just daydreaming, unwilling to put some effort and energy into the accomplishment of that dream, or are we headed on a path of seeing those daring dreams become realities?

Exercise: Write down a dream that inspires and excites you. It could be something small, like a vacation or an achievement ... or it could be something huge, like your purpose in life. Now think about that dream and see if your heart is right now more focused on daydreaming and wishful thinking, or if you are actively engaged with ideas and plans of how to see that dream become a reality.

DAY EIGHT
DREAMS AND GOALS

#2: **HEALTHY** DISCONTENT

If you and I are to give expression to our full potential, we need to have a real dream, a daring dream, a big dream … one that will challenge and drive us onward.

We have talked before about the differences between daydreaming and a daring dream. The daydream relies on luck and the daring dream relies on discipline. The daydream focuses on the destination and the daring dream focuses on the journey. We have invested some time evaluating our own dreams to see if they are more on the side of daydreaming or if we have found a place inside of us that connects with the deeper, daring, real dream.

Here's another way to tell the difference: the daydream cultivates unhealthy expectations, but the daring dream cultivates healthy discontent.

Just pause here for a moment.

Yes, I am suggesting that healthy discontent is okay. My goal in life, at least, *one* of my goals in life, is to be filled with joy and happiness all the time. However, there are times when I realize that I am not fulfilling my potential. There are times when I realize that I need to do more than what I'm doing, or I need to do something differently than the way I'm doing it. When those kinds of realizations come, I am discontented with where I am, but I'm still contented with the overall experience of life.

This can be an ambiguous distinction to make, but when we learn to make it, then life becomes an adventurous journey and a real joy to live. Is there such a thing as unhealthy discontent? Of course there is. If our spirit of discontent pulls us to become bitter, jaded, entitled, jealous, or selfish, it is certainly unhealthy. The goal is to allow those feelings of discontent to pull us to become stronger, motivated, focused, determined, and passionate about becoming all that we are created to be.

Unhealthy expectations, on the other hand, come from daydreaming. When we engage in wishful thinking without any plan or drive to move towards the dream, we can allow unhealthy expectations to creep in. We can get caught up in believing that "hoping" is all it will take to see a dream realized. And if we do nothing to move towards our dream, we will almost always end up disappointed.

So the healthy discontent, then, propels us towards our dream. It gives us reason and motivation to make changes and plans – it gives us fuel to add to the fire of our daring dream. And as our passion ignites, we cannot help but move towards the dream and towards becoming all that we are created to be.

Exercise: Identify one area of your life where you feel a healthy discontent (meaning you feel motivated and passionate to make a positive change). Then identify one area of your life where you feel an unhealthy discontent (meaning you feel jealous, defeated, or entitled). How can you transition the unhealthy discontent into something more positive?

DAY NINE
DREAMS AND GOALS

#3: **FEARING** OUR DREAMS

When we embrace our daring dreams as something to pursue and not just to think about, we are frequently met with the roadblock of fear. Fear is a powerful distraction and if we are not careful and deliberate in handling it, it can keep us at a standstill instead of in a rhythm of forward movement towards our dream.

What about you? What are the fears that get in the way of your daring dream? Are you afraid that you won't be able to accomplish it? Or are you fearful that you *will* be able to accomplish it, but then you won't know how to handle it? Maybe you are afraid that you don't really deserve it. I understand all these fears … and I have felt them all about various dreams that I have pursued in my life. These questions are worth asking, and these fears are worth facing, because the fact is that the daring dream will always be bigger than these fears.

Here's a big one that can paralyze us: sometimes we become afraid that our dreams do not match up with our abilities. We believe that a desire in our hearts is an unfair and hopeless desire, because we do not have the capacity to make it happen. My observation about this is that frequently, almost always, they *do* match up. If you really know what it is that you want to do, if it's a daring dream, a challenging dream, then my observation is that—for the most part—the talents and abilities to do that are already within you. They are a part of who you are. And the fact that those talents and abilities exist within you is a major reason that your dream was born in the first place.

Whatever our fears are, they can destroy any forward movement towards our dream. The goal, then, is to begin to overcome the fear.

Here's one way to begin to overcome it: identify your fear. When I begin to understand what my fear is, I begin to find ways to overcome it. When I'm willing to actually get specific about the fear, to verbalize it, to talk about it, that is a giant step toward overpowering it.

Exercise: Write down the specific fears you have about the daring dreams in your life.

DAY TEN
DREAMS AND GOALS

#4: **FACING** THE CRITICS

In the pursuit of our daring dreams, we will always find critics along the way. This is a touchy subject, because oftentimes those critical people are friends or even family members. They are people who for all the right reasons and all of the best intentions are concerned about you and your dreams. They attempt to give you perspective and wisdom that they feel you cannot have on your own ... but in the process, they can become roadblocks on your journey towards accomplishing your dreams. Too often, they speak from the depths of their own fears and shortcomings that became the barricades in their own lives.

People are made uncomfortable by the one who has that daring, radical dream for life, that challenging dream, the vision, the hope of great things tomorrow. It's oftentimes unsettling to the one who has no dreams or only daydreams. When they think about you achieving your dream, it begins to move them out of their comfort zone, because they have to reevaluate all the reasons why they are not pursuing their own.

And we can have empathy for those people who have to battle their own comfort zones and the pull of their own dreams on their hearts. We don't need to scoff at their lack of belief or belittle their opinions in a rude manner. However, we must guard our hearts from buying into the same lie that they have bought into. Whatever their lie is, you can recognize it and move onward, confident that your daring dream is worth fighting through the critics and those who choose to judge or be controlled by fear.

Remember that the intention of the critic is usually good. They are trying to save you from pain of embarrassment or failure. However, what the critic usually fails to realize is that pain and embarrassment and failure are all parts of the path that will lead to the eventual fulfillment of your dream! Nobody has ever fully achieved a daring dream without walking through some pain and embarrassment and failure.

So, have grace for your critics, and hold on to the hope that perhaps your example of pursuing your own dream despite your fears and doubts will inspire them to make a similar choice in their own life. Perhaps one day they will cease to be a critic and become a running mate. That would be a day to celebrate indeed.

Exercise: *Identify the loudest critic in your life. What is the lie they are trying to get you to buy into? How can you combat that lie with truth?*

DAY ELEVEN
DREAMS AND GOALS

#5: **WRITE DOWN** YOUR GOALS

Today we are going to think very specifically about the benefit of writing our goals down. I have discovered that until I came to the point where I was willing to crystallize my goals by writing them down, I had not made the emotional commitment to the goals that is hugely beneficial for their successful completion. There is something powerful in the act of writing down our goals, almost as though we are promising ourselves that these thoughts in our minds are more than just thoughts; they are objectives that we are willing to work towards.

I am sure many of you who have listened to the *Dynamic Living* seminar have heard me share my early experiences with writing things down. I was extremely skeptical that it would have *any* effect at all on my ability to accomplish goals in my life. In fact, I remember a number of arguments that I had over the course of those years, discussing the value of writing goals down. I believed that perhaps there was only a certain sort of personality type that would benefit from such a practice.

I am still not convinced that I know all of the reasons why it makes a difference, but I will tell you that I am certainly convinced that it *does make a difference*. It may, in fact, be essential. When we take the time and emotional energy to really think our goals through enough so that we can write them down, it turns our roaming thoughts into concrete intentions. The benefits of having specific, concrete goals to work towards are always significant.

Another thing I have discovered about the act of writing things down is that it gives me the chance to continually clarify my thoughts about them. The first time I write a goal down, it might not be the exact way that I want to say it. It might not be the precise thing I want to achieve, or it might be said in a way that focuses my energy in a less-than-ideal direction. When I go through the process of writing, reading, and re-writing, it helps me crystalize the goal in a way that makes its eventual completion extremely fulfilling. Another observation about this process is that the time I invest developing the goal spurs my thinking about how to accomplish it and it also leads me towards actually taking action.

So I encourage you to write down your goals. Just give it a try, even if you are skeptical of the value. Write them, read them daily, rewrite them from time to time. You will discover that the mental focus and clarity that comes with this practice is more than worth the effort.

Exercise: *Write down 3 goals that you would like to achieve in the next year.*

DAY TWELVE
DREAMS AND GOALS

#6: **PAYING** THE PRICE

Once we have taken the time to dream BIG dreams, and we have put in the effort to write down specific goals, we have to take the next step, which is to ask ourselves the question: *Am I willing to pay the price?*

This is a defining and crucial question in the process of achieving our goals. Goal setting is not a mystical process whereby things come into being in our lives with no effort on our part. Quite the contrary! Goal setting takes hard work and dedication. Setting a goal is not rubbing a magic lamp; setting a goal is making a promise to ourselves that we are willing to do whatever it takes in order to achieve the objective that we desire.

Once we decide what it is that we want, define it clearly and specifically, and write it down, we arrive at the more difficult step in the process. This is the point where we ask ourselves some questions about the goal. *Will I pay the price for this? Am I willing to do what it is going to take to accomplish this goal? Am I will to invest the time this will take? Am I willing to invest the physical and emotional energy this will take? Am I willing to invest the money this will take? Is the end result of achieving this goal worth the effort that it will take to get there?*

Only you can answer these questions for yourself. What might be worth it to one person might not be worth it to someone else. For example, losing 10 pounds will require something of you. It will require exercise, diet change, and self-control. Losing 10 pounds will also benefit you. It will help you look better, feel better, and be healthier. Only you can decide whether the benefits outweigh the price.

If you discover that you have set a goal that requires a price higher than you are willing to pay, the next step is to adjust the goal. For example, let's say your goal is to complete a book project within the next 6 months. After careful consideration, you realize that in order to do that, you will have to sacrifice too much time with your family. Your life will be out of balance and the rewards of finishing your book project will be lessened because of the price of losing too many special moments with your family. Does this mean failure? Do you then abandon your book project altogether? No! You simply adjust the goal. Perhaps you give yourself a year to complete the book project, and you deliberately schedule writing time and family time. Now the rewards will be so much greater, because the price was worth the investment.

We dare not embark towards a goal that we know has a price we are absolutely not willing to pay. That will lead to failure in multiple areas of life and probably to a lot of pain. If we pay only *part* of the price and see little to no results, we begin a process of self-doubt that is difficult to reverse. Instead, we are wise if we will evaluate the price. Once we have decided that we are willing to put the effort and time and heart into our goals, then all that remains is to move confidently towards them.

Exercise: *Assess your 3 goals from yesterday. Are you willing to pay the price? If not, adjust them so that the price they will require is something that you are willing to pay.*

DAY THIRTEEN
DREAMS AND GOALS

#7: **CHECKPOINTS**

Today I want to encourage us to establish checkpoints as we begin to work towards the goals we have set. Pre-established intervals to assess our efforts are powerful in their ability to keep us on track. The times when I am most effective, when I accomplish the most, and when I get closest to the goals that I have established are the times when I am deliberate about setting frequent checkpoints. The times when I miss the mark or fall short of the goal are the times when I actually go through the process of setting the goal but then never really track it until the deadline is near or even past.

So, I believe that frequent checkpoints for our goals are crucial in the process of their achievement. In fact, if we want to be the most effective, if we are pursuing a goal that is extremely important to us, it really should be daily checkpoints.

At the beginning of every day, take a look at what the day has in store for you. Read your goals. Ask yourself these questions: *What are the things that I will do today that will bring me further along the road to accomplishing this goal? What can I do today that will take me closer? What must I avoid doing today that would take me further away from my goal?* Then, at the close of the day, read your goals again. Take a look at what you have actually done to see whether or not you have taken the necessary steps towards the accomplishment of your goals.

Upon reading this, you might get the feeling that this idea of checkpoints sounds like a lot of extra time and energy involved. Well, you are right! This will take an extra degree of focus, commitment, and consistency. However, it will give the accountability, motivation, and productivity that you need in order to complete the goal that means so much to you.

The fact is that while setting checkpoints and sticking with them daily takes time and energy, it takes an even greater degree of time and energy to stop and start your engine or to steam full ahead on some days and then be listless for days or weeks or months at a time. By applying the technique of daily engagement and assessment, you will keep yourself consistent and thereby end up *saving* yourself time and energy.

There may be goals that don't require daily attention. For those, determine what interval of checkpoints will help to keep you on track. Will it be weekly? Will it be monthly? Or will you just hope for the best? I trust it is not the last one for you, because my observation is that that one doesn't work very well at all.

This book is about all daily discipline: little things that we can do consistently that will make a huge difference. Checkpoints for our goals are one of those disciplines that will transform our lives.

Exercise: *Consider how the idea of checkpoints can fit into your schedule. Write down your intentions about checkpoints for your goals.*

DAY FOURTEEN
DO IT NOW!

In the *Dynamic Living* seminar that I have taught for the last 40 years or so, one of the 10 principles of success I have always talked about is "action". The summary statement for this simple but powerful principle is: *Do It Now*.

I think this principle of action could almost be considered the *ultimate* daily discipline … do it now!

If we were to come to the place where every single day we actually took action on something in our lives that would lead us towards growth and change and our dreams, imagine the productive, energetic, successful, charismatic people we would be! Picture the massive change we would see in our lives over time as we daily take action that moves us towards our dreams. Think of the momentum we would create with that forward movement.

There is a major difference between planning to take action and actually taking the action. Many components go into the planning and they are all important and good … but *only* if we follow through on that planning with action. If we don't act on our plan, then it's really all for nothing. In fact, taking action without planning at all is often better than continually being in the process of planning.

Many have used the phrase "beginning is half done", meaning that once we actually begin doing something, we've already more than half completed the mental work of getting it done. The problem for many of us as we work towards accomplishing our goals is not that we can't do it. Rather, it is that we often *don't get started* doing it at all. We never actually begin, or perhaps we take a small step, meet some opposition, and then never push through it towards continued action.

If you have something you want to accomplish, you need to get moving and *do it now*. If you aren't sure exactly how to do it, just put one foot in front of the other and start going. Invest the time necessary for the planning but do not allow that to be a substitute for time invested in the doing, and you will discover that the lessons you learn in the doing will teach you things you could have never understood in the planning.

As we learn to make action a daily discipline rather than a sporadic burst of activity, we will find ourselves on a swift and sure path of achieving our goals and moving closer to our dreams.

Exercise: *Write down one important action step you can take today. And then … Do It Now!*

DAY FIFTEEN
GRATEFULNESS

I'm reminded frequently of a simple yet powerful song that I used to sing as a youngster. The main lyrics said, "Count your many blessings, name them one by one."[2]

It was a song that always reminded me that life is better lived when we have a spirit of gratefulness working in our lives every day. It reminded me, and still does remind me, to look for the good, recognize the good, celebrate the good, and speak of the good.

I remember back to the days of doing the *Daily Disciplines* podcast. My mother, who was 97 years old at the time, lived with us at our home in Florida. One day, she came into my office and said, "Well, I listened twice today."

I said, "To what?"

"To the *Daily Disciplines*," she replied.

Then, she said something to me that was so uplifting and encouraging, I'll never forget it. "Yes, I listened twice today. You know, in the last 3 days I've accomplished more than I have in the last several weeks, because I've been listening to and doing what the *Daily Disciplines* program says to do."

The reality was that my mother, who taught me many of the great things about living life effectively, was then—at her age—listening to my teaching on a daily basis. Now here's what I recall about the power of her words. She was grateful for my investment into her life. Instead of just recognizing that gratitude, she made a deliberate effort to thank me, to share her gratefulness. And because of that, I became encouraged, inspired, and motivated to continue my efforts. And therefore, I felt gratefulness as well.

It's a simple story. We all could probably tell countless stories of people who have shared a word of gratitude or thanks for something we have done. But what about all the times when we haven't chosen to be grateful? Or the times when we have felt grateful and yet kept it to ourselves?

Think about how much more of a beautiful place the world becomes when we approach life looking for ways to be grateful and for ways to express that gratefulness. See, it's not only about the difference that something or someone has made in your life; it's about the difference that you can make back in their lives by thanking them for it.

Exercise: *Write down some things for which you're grateful. If there's somebody you could to say "thank you" or "I appreciate you" to, then do it.*

DAY SIXTEEN
COMPARISON

This may be a radical statement, but I'm going to make it anyhow: Comparison is the single most damaging process in human relationships.

If we could cease comparing ourselves with each other, it would solve almost all relationship problems. Comparison causes brokenness in relationships, brings marriages to an end, propels nations to war, and perpetuates constant bickering and fighting among people. In spite of the fact that our society has positively progressed in every other area of human development - scientific knowledge, athletic ability, technological advancement, etc. – we have not ever been able to progress very far in the area of human relationships.

It just seems to me, from all the years of experience I have in dealing with people, that if we could get this one thing right, it would begin to straighten out all the other problems with people.

Here is my observation about most human relationships: we constantly compare ourselves to others. We are geared towards competition, being the best, being number one. And when the value we place on ourselves is based on who we are in comparison to someone else, conflict or jealousy or competition or depression will arise ... every time.

Somehow, we have been conditioned to believe this comparison is necessary. We delude ourselves into thinking that if we can just be better than *somebody* else, we will be that much closer to the fulfillment of our potential.

I need to come to the place where I accept the fact that I am a worthwhile human being. I am worth loving. I am somebody. Because I am somebody, I have a unique purpose in life. I don't have to be defensive about it, nor do I have to be prideful about it. I just need to pursue excellence by using my talents and abilities to accomplish what I am designed to do.

This realization of the value of every individual, including myself, was influenced by many of the informal mentors I had in the early days. Some of them became personal friends of mind, and their influence was even more profound. Dave Grant was one of those personal friends. In his book, *The Ultimate Power*, he opened my eyes to a statement that I have shared with all who would listen: "Our self-worth is a GIVEN. What we've been working so hard to get, we've already got: A SELF WORTH LOVING."[3]

Exercise: *Write down one relationship that could be improved by dropping your compulsion to compare. Make a few notes on what the improved relationship would look like.*

DAY SEVENTEEN
CHOICES

#1: **SMALL** CHOICES

Human beings have a truly marvelous amount of potential. I invested a great deal of time in years past learning how much we are capable of doing and accomplishing. While it is important to understand and appreciate all the talents we have, our focus today is more related to how we *use* our abilities.

The fact is that it really all comes down to the choices we make.

We are all overflowing with potential, yet some achieve amazing things and others struggle to keep their heads above water. What makes the difference? I believe that it is our choices. Some of those choices are large, full-scale life decisions, while others are small choices that simply pave the pathway to our success or failure. We make choices about career, marriage, family, homes, finances—and those are the big ones. Those are the ones that we already know will alter the course of our life one way or another. It is important to approach those choices with a solid plan for making good decisions.

But let's think for a moment about the small choices—the things that don't necessarily seem in the moment like they are going to have a lasting impact on your life. Things like choosing kindness or anger in the middle of a disagreement, or choosing to go to the gym rather than sleep in on a Saturday. Things like waking up in the morning with a deliberate intent to choose a positive attitude rather than a discouraged one, or choosing to invest some time with your kids rather than answering one more email; these small choices are constantly presented to us.

We don't have space or time to list out every single choice that you will be presented with throughout your lifetime. Choices are endless; you make them every moment of every day. The key for today is to remember that *you do have a choice*. You always have an option for how you will handle yourself in any given situation. And here's a fact that can make a huge difference as you make choices in your life: successful, happy people do not base their choices on their emotions. They base their choices on what is best for the fulfillment of their potential.

So what will we choose today, tomorrow? My hope is that today we will choose to think about our choices.

Exercise: What is one deliberate choice you can make today that will take you farther along the path of becoming the person you are created to be?

DAY EIGHTEEN
CHOICES

#2: **BALANCE** IS A CHOICE

Today we will continue talking about choices, and specifically about balance. In our world today, this can be one of the most difficult paths to navigate. Many of us feel that we are left having to choose success in one area of life at the expense of another area. When we get caught up in this way of thinking, we miss considering the fact that we do, in fact, have another choice.

We can choose balance.

When talking about balance, I've often told the story of the body builder I met at a speaking engagement. I asked him what type of commitment was required to get his body to look the way it did and he explained that it meant being at the gym 7 days a week for many years. Then I asked if it was worth it. He quickly responded that it had not been worth it, and began to explain how his family had fallen apart because he spent so much time working on his physical self. I tell this story here to illustrate that the cost of certain goals may include sacrifice in other areas.

It is my belief that the things that are really worth attaining in life are only worth it if we can achieve balance along the way to attaining them. If we destroy other pieces of our lives in the pursuit of one thing, we will never feel satisfied or whole in our achievement.

How then do you achieve balance? This is where you have to make specific choices. The choices need to be based upon what your priorities are. We will talk in detail about priorities, but it really comes down to determining what is most important to you and then holding yourself to that list of priorities. However, there may be seasons of life where priorities need to be shuffled a bit for the sake of a press towards a goal. You don't need to beat yourself up about these seasons. You simply need to remember to care for the other areas of your life as well.

The balance will come when you make decisions about the priorities for a given season of your life, and then you hold yourself to them. If you are making decisions in the moment, based on what is right in front of you rather than what you hold to be most important, you will easily shift out of balance.

This is a skill that can take years to develop, but it is one well worth mastering. There is a unique freedom that comes from a balanced life, and I encourage all of us to work on cultivating balance in our lives. When we choose balance, when that is a focus of our attention, we can achieve it.

Exercise: What is one deliberate choice you can make today that will allow you to feel that you are taking a balanced approach to your day?

DAY NINETEEN
CHOICES

#3: **RESPONSIBILITY** IS A CHOICE

Today we are investing our time in talking about the fact that responsibility is a choice. This area is significant, and in some cases choosing responsibility can be really hard. Making this choice can radically change your life, but it requires a strength of character and a maturity that our society at best ignores and oftentimes tends to undermine.

Situations, events, and occurrences will happen throughout the course of our lives. These instances might be good or they might be bad. We always have a choice of how we will respond. We are, after all, *response-able*. If it's a bad situation we can choose to assign blame and be a victim of circumstances outside of our control. Or we can choose to be *response-able* and control what we can: our response.

The best way for me to illustrate this point is with an example. Jim is a hardworking guy. He always meets his deadlines, puts in overtime when needed, and helps the members of his team finish their projects. One day, Jim's company is bought out and he comes in to work to find he is being laid off. Initially, there's shock, hurt, and uncertainty, but there comes a point where Jim has a choice. He didn't have a choice in being laid off, but he does have a choice in how he responds to what has happened.

He could choose to be a victim and his thoughts would probably take him from anger to depression as he floats along, being tossed about by the circumstances of life. It could even erupt into some sort of breakdown or workplace violence. Or, he could choose to be *response-able*; not for the loss of a job but for the life he is living. He could choose to learn from the experience, expect good things, and move forward towards finding a new job.

I know this may sound harsh and I'm not suggesting that when a life event like this happens that it isn't upsetting. It very much is. That being said, we can only control what we can control: our response.

There are also times in life where we *are* responsible for bad things that happen to us. Poor choices do lead to hard consequences, and there is no getting around that fact. We will all make poor choices from time to time. When we do make a poor choice, the fastest way to turn things back around towards something positive is to simply take responsibility for the choice, rather than blaming others. If Jim had been fired because of sloppy work or inappropriate behavior, it would do him little good to blame his firing on his employers or co-workers. The *response-able* choice is to own up to the mistakes, and then move on towards something better.

Responsibility for our actions is a choice. If more of us would make this choice, our world would be a far better place.

Exercise: *Is there an area in your life where you feel like a victim? How can you choose a response-able attitude instead?*

DAY TWENTY
CHOICES

#4: **HAPPINESS** IS A CHOICE

One of the core parts of the *Dynamic Living* seminar is the statement: "You always have a choice. You can choose to be happy or you can choose to be grumpy. It's always better, it's always smarter, it's always wiser to choose to be happy." While this may seem like a small decision that we must make over and over each day—or even each hour or minute—it can make all the difference.

You always have a choice. Think of a time when you've encountered someone who is grumpy or gloomy or angry. How was that interaction? Chances are that it wasn't a very good one. Now, think of a time when you encountered a happy person. How was that experience? More than likely it was far more encouraging and you came away a little bit better for having encountered that individual.

You always have a choice. Suppose you are working with someone on a project and they make an error. Will you become upset and unload all your anger and venom on them for the mistake? Will you eviscerate them with your words? And if this is your choice, what then happens to the project and to the team? Or, you could go another route and simply be kind and work with them to correct the error. Now, how different is the outcome likely to be? Radically.

There are countless scenarios we could consider, but there would be a common thread in them all: it's always better, it's always smarter, it's always wiser to choose to be happy.

Now … it's not always easier. Quite the opposite sometimes! Happiness is rarely our first reaction to a problem. I've come to recognize that there are circumstances of life that can break our hearts and defeat our spirits for a time. I have had family and friends experience terrible tragedies. I have experienced some myself. I'm not suggesting that you shouldn't grieve or mourn the tragedies of life. I'm not suggesting that life is just blue skies and smooth sailing if we just "choose to be happy".

What I am suggesting is that we have a choice even in the tragedies. Do we let them define us, derail us, and defeat us? Or do we choose to look for the good? Do we realize that life is still worth living, dreams are still worth chasing, and happiness is still worth choosing?

We always have a choice.

Exercise: Think of a situation in your life where you are having a hard time choosing to be happy. Write down 3 good things that can come from that situation.

DAY TWENTY-ONE
CHOICES

#5: **FORGIVENESS** IS A CHOICE

Forgiveness is a choice that sets us free from the mindsets, feelings, and habits of behavior that bind us to our past and limit us in our experiences of today.

That's a big statement to swallow, I know. The first part of it, *"forgiveness is a choice"*, is particularly difficult to get our heads around, especially in situations when we have clearly been hurt. There are times when people will be wrong. You know it. They know it. God knows it. And so ... how can we simply choose to forgive them? What about our justifiable feelings in the matter? What about an apology from our offenders?

I remember the day that my dad became gridlocked in this struggle to choose forgiveness. He was facing some major challenges in his life, and he said to me, "If they would just ask me to forgive them, I would." His bitterness trapped him, and it devastated his life. Literally. He could not choose to forgive, and the resentment destroyed everything he had left, including his health.

My dad needed his offenders to acknowledge their wrongdoing before he could forgive it. In his mind, it was about them recognizing what they had done. *It was about them.*

But the reality is that true forgiveness is never about the other person. It is not about the offense, it is not about punishment or vindication, it is not about proving that I am right. It is never really about *them*… it is always about me. It is about releasing anger and bitterness and blame and embracing grace instead.

We can make the choice about *which way to go* on the journey to forgive. We can make the choice to travel through life, hiding bitterness and blame until we finally feel the other person has paid their debt and felt the necessary penitence, and then decide to forgive them. But this choice will lock us into our past and limit anything beautiful we can create or become in our present.

There is another direction to take on this journey of forgiveness. We can choose to let it go and walk away from the hurt. We can choose to release the need to see the other person pay. We can choose to let go of our need to hear their apology and to know that they have fully felt the weight of their wrongdoing. And when we do release the need for those things, we find ourselves free.

Who in your life do you need to forgive? Maybe it's another person, someone who has wronged you. You know who it is. Or maybe, just maybe, that forgiveness needs to go inward. Maybe you just need to forgive yourself. Think about it. Is there something you feel like you still need to feel punishment and shame for?

Forgiveness is a choice. It's a choice that sets us free from the mindsets, feelings, and habits of behavior that bind us to our past and limit us in our experience of today.

Exercise: *Write down the person in your life that you most need to forgive. Write down how you will feel differently once you no longer possess the need to see a price paid for that offense.*

DAY TWENTY-TWO
CHOICES

#6: **LOVE** IS A CHOICE

The most powerful choice you will ever make in your life is the choice to love.

During the *Dynamic Living* seminar at Circle A, we devote one of the longest sessions to the topic of love. I have consistently and regularly received feedback that this portion of the seminar is incredibly impactful and paradigm shifting for the campers who attend.

In the world we live in, love is distorted to be something it is not. Our music sends the message that we "fall in love", and our movies give us the idea that we just might meet someone who is our perfect "soul mate". Unfortunately these same media sources seem to indicate that it is about as easy to "fall out of love" as it is to "fall in love". Although these emotions and experiences do occur, many buy into the idea that these feelings are the basis for a relationship of love. They believe that if these emotions cease to exist, then the love must have fizzled and died. If we believe this, we are often left searching for this lasting euphoria. We are left disillusioned when we discover the more difficult parts of all human relationships.

The thesis of the love seminar at Circle A is that we are all inherently lovable. We derive a worth and value that is not based on anything we do or become. It is based solely on the fact that we are beautiful, unique, individual creations of God. When we arrive at the conclusion that we are all inherently lovable, then for us to love anyone … all we have to do is *decide*. There isn't anything we have to do; there are no conditions or expectations to meet that make us lovable.

Before Susan and I were married, she would often ask me what I loved about her. I refused to give her an answer. I didn't want to put a condition on my love for her. As an example, if I said that I loved her hair, and then something happened one day that made her lose her hair, she could begin to doubt my love for her. At first this was somewhat upsetting to Susan, but as we talked more and I explained why, she understood and deeply appreciated the fact that my love for her is a choice. We developed ways to complement each other without it creating conditional love.

This concept of love being a *decision* extends to far more relationships than marriage. Is there something your kids could do that would negate your love for them? How about your parents? Or your friends?

Today, let's think about what our relationships would look like if our love were truly unconditional. Let's think about what our world would look like if we treated people as though their worth was inherent in their existence and not based on living up to a set of criteria. Let's think about the way we love ourselves too. What sort of criteria are we placing on our own worth?

Exercise: Think about a relationship in your life that is based on conditional love. What steps could you take to make that love unconditional?

DAY TWENTY-THREE
A HEALTHY DIET

During the *Dynamic Living* seminar, I devote a portion of time talking about how our minds process input and then I urge everyone who will hear me to deeply question what they are *feeding their minds*. We are so focused on healthy, clean eating in our society today – no sugar substitutes, no GMOs, no HFCS – the list goes on. But how much do we pay attention to the diets of our minds and our hearts and our souls? I think this is a truly important question to ask, so we'll ask it of ourselves today.

In our culture, there is no shortage of input. We have access to virtually every book ever written and we can read or listen to them. There is a constant stream of movies and television and video clips playing on every device we care to look at. Music of every sort is available instantaneously. Social media has captured our time and attention at an alarming rate, creating a wide-open forum for any and all input to be force-fed to our minds. We can have it all, any time, any place. With all this supply, we know our minds will not go hungry. In fact, we have become so overrun with input that our minds have become rather gluttonous with the intake.

This is not a reason to panic or to throw out every media device that we own – but it is a reason to more closely monitor what we are exposing our minds to. Our brains are always on—continuously taking in data and storing it. In order for us to be the best versions of ourselves, we need to monitor this input and regulate it. This is no different than our diet. We owe it to our own mental health to restrict the amount of garbage we consume.

We need to ask ourselves the difficult questions and we must stop believing the lie that we are immune to the influences of negative media. Do the television shows and movies that you watch enrich your life or do they add to a storehouse of fear and worry? Do the books you read give you healthy mental nutrition or are they filled with empty filth? Does the time you invest on social media help to build relationships and encourage you or does it breed feelings of mistrust, fear, envy, and negativity? Does the music you listen to uplift and inspire you or does it send you into an emotional tailspin? And what about your relationships—do the friends you spend your time with fill your mind with healthy encouragement and truth?

I realize these questions sound harsh. The fact is that all of these categories have healthy versions that can fill you with good mental nutrition. There are great movies and music and books and friends. Social media can absolutely be a useful and encouraging part of your life. But *only* if you deliberately control the diet of what you are feeding your mind.

Exercise: *What parts of your mental consumption need to go on a diet? What healthy alternatives can you add to your life to build proper mental nutrition?*

DAY TWENTY-FOUR
FLEXIBILITY

I often enjoy the skylines of major cities and marvel at how tall the buildings are. When I see buildings like the Empire State Building in New York, they remind me of the marvels of modern engineering. The Empire State Building is made of a steel frame and is on top of a solid concrete foundation. Here's what isn't obvious: the steel tower is not rigid. It sways a bit. It has to have some flexibility to it or it will crumble with a slight increase in winds. Things that are rigid break faster than things that can bend.

Why do we have to be flexible? Well, as we have said before, life is full of circumstances that could break us if we are not prepared to handle them. Our plans, no matter how perfectly mapped out and executed, rarely succeed without some adjustments and midcourse corrections. If we are too rigid with the execution of our well-intentioned plans, we can easily be derailed by any circumstance that comes along which makes our original path impossible. If we are not willing to be flexible and adjust our original plan, we can become defeated, jaded, bitter, and accepting of our failure. We break.

I'm not sure who originated this phrase, but my good friend Jim Dornan often used to say it. "You have to have your goals in concrete and your plans in sand." The goal doesn't change, but how you get there might have to. In fact, it probably will have to change in greater or lesser degrees. If that variation in strategy derails you, then you will always be on a slower and harder path to achievement.

When I am preparing the leadership team at Circle A each summer, the topic of flexibility is one that we always give attention to. This is an imperative skill for our staff to learn. The fact is that things will not always run on schedule. We may move one day's events to a different day because of weather or other circumstances. When this happens, it is crucial that the staff is able to adjust on the fly and jump right into the new events we are doing, versus bemoaning the fact that they prepared for something else. While this is sometimes a difficult and frustrating skill to learn, it makes a huge difference in the morale of the staff, the enjoyment of the campers, and the effectiveness of the session. I am convinced that members of our leadership team who have truly embraced this trait will continue to be highly successful in their chosen professions and in their relationships.

We need to be flexible—adjusting to overcome circumstances and respecting the teams of people we work with. Remember, the *goal* does not need to be fickle, shifting in the wake of circumstance and emotion. It is the *plan and execution* that needs to remain flexible, so that the goal can be achieved.

Exercise: *What current plan that you are trying to execute could benefit from some flexibility? What would that flexibility look like? What would it help you to achieve?*

DAY TWENTY-FIVE
PERSEVERANCE

I'm not sure if you know this about me, but I enjoy words. There was a time in my life when I learned that words are powerful, and so I invested a lot of time learning new words and their meanings. I tell you this because when I start to teach about "perseverance", I find that it is often confused with "endurance". Endurance is a good thing, but it's more about surviving. Endurance is vital to the accomplishing of a goal, but it is more about developing the stamina to persist through the difficult situations of life. Persevering, however, is about *thriving*. It means when there is a stumbling point, challenge, or problem, we adapt and keep moving forward. We are resilient, and we grow and change as we keep moving toward our goal.

In my experience, the seeds of perseverance are sown when we first establish the goal. Persistence is one of the principles of success in the *Dynamic Living* seminar. The statement that goes with it is, "I will … until". Once the course of action is set, I will continue down that path, adjusting when necessary, until I reach my goal.

There is another principle of success that goes hand in hand with perseverance, and that is visualization. The phrase I use to teach about this principle is, "Get a clear mental picture of what you want, fill it with emotion, and hang on". In building up this emotion, we have a source of inspiration and passion to draw from when the challenges come. This emotion is the fuel for our perseverance.

When the challenges come, and it's a fact of life that they will, perseverance means we will find a way around them. We will find the good, extract it, and then navigate around the bad and on to the goal.

I need to add a few words of caution here. We are talking about challenges and problems. I'm not addressing catastrophes. Sometimes there are devastating circumstances that are so big that we cannot so simply navigate around them. Such a situation may be better served by enduring until we come to a place where we are ready to dream again. A long-range, big-picture camera angle is of tremendous benefit in coming to that place where we can begin to see the future with hope.

I invite you today to take some time to think about the ways that you can persevere through your circumstances and obstacles. Remember that the fuel of this perseverance comes from a deep passion for the purpose that you are pursuing.

Exercise: *What is the purpose that you are persevering for? What are some obstacles that are in your way?*

DAY TWENTY-SIX
PROCRASTINATION

#1: **INTRODUCTION**

Can I be real honest with you? Well, I suppose I can be since you aren't here to stop me. I really, really dislike the topic of procrastination. I don't particularly enjoy writing about it or speaking about it or even thinking about it. Because the fact is … I struggle with procrastination.

And yet, I recognize that the seasons in my life where I am deliberately thinking about it or teaching about it or writing about it … I struggle a lot less! So perhaps the first lesson of the day is that a simple awareness of a tendency to procrastinate is an important part in overcoming it.

With that said, today we will begin a series of several days that will help us to become aware of places that we procrastinate and of things we can do to be better about it. I don't want to lose part of my life on wasteful pursuits and my guess is that you don't either. Once we have wasted time, it cannot be regained. So let's think about some ways that we can be better about persisting rather than procrastinating.

There are things that need to be addressed in my life, today, now. There are things in your life that need to be addressed now too, and we cannot evade the responsibility of those things by simply putting them off. It is amazing to me how many of us continue to put things off until we arrive at what we believe will be a better time to do it. We convince ourselves that there will come a more convenient time, a time when we are better prepared, a time when there are not so many other things vying for our attention.

Why do we do this? How do we recognize it when we do it? Is there anything we can do about it, or is it just part of the human experience? What about the times when there are "legitimate" excuses for putting things off? How do we motivate ourselves to do the things that we are procrastinating about?

The experts tell us that most all of us procrastinate, and many of us do it chronically, habitually. In fact, according to *Psychology Today*, 20% of people identity themselves as chronic procrastinators.[4] Hopefully you do not fall into the chronic category, but I believe that everyone has room for improvement in this area.

So … let's get to it!

Exercise: *Evaluate your to-do list. Is there anything on there that you have been waiting for perfect conditions to begin? Is there one step you could take towards it … today?*

DAY TWENTY-SEVEN
PROCRASTINATION

#2: WHAT IS **PROCRASTINATION**?

Procrastination is a habitual way of fraudulently justifying to ourselves that a particular endeavor should not, does not need to, or cannot be started now. In the attempt, then, to validate this proposition, procrastinators will fill their time with other tasks of lesser importance so that the primary task can be avoided.

Sir Isaac Newton said that a body at rest stays at rest, and a body in motion stays in motion.[5] My observation is that this is especially true in the case of procrastination. Tasks or challenges tend to remain at rest until they are put into motion, and then they frequently remain in motion once they are initiated. It is the energy required to begin the motion that we tend to struggle with.

So how can we get into motion and avoid procrastination?

First, we must determine our reason for procrastinating. There are many different reasons we do this and we don't have the time to unpack them all here. But there are some categories of reasons and that is what we will consider today. Dr. Joseph Ferrari, Ph.D., associate professor of psychology at De Paul University in Chicago, is one of the world's leading experts on procrastination. He identifies 3 types of procrastinators, which I will give my thoughts on today.[6]

The first category is the ***thrill seekers***. These procrastinators oftentimes wait for the adrenaline rush that comes when a deadline is approaching. There is an energy that comes with this adrenaline that can help propel things into motion and complete them quickly. I can't say that you shouldn't do this if I have done it myself, but I do know this: if it leads me down a road of procrastination, then it is not an effective strategy. Although I might know that I can write a speech the night before I am meant to deliver it, that does not mean I should spend all the rest of the nights in that week just watching TV and wasting my life away. It would be far better to be productive with my time and to complete the work on the speech with plenty of time to spare.

The second major category to talk about is the ***avoiders***. These procrastinators are driven by the desire to avoid things, rather than to achieve things. They may wish to avoid discomfort, hard work, the unknown, risk … the list could go on. Frequently they wish to avoid tasks because of fear of failure or even fear of success, and this type of avoidance is usually based around the concern of what others will think of them. Avoiders usually fill their time with things that distract them from what they really need to be doing: things like housework, television, Facebook, etc. There is certainly a point to be made, though I will not try to make it here, about how often our technological devices provide us a distraction and incite procrastination.

The final major category is the ***indecisive procrastinators***. There are many people who really hate decision-making and feel that procrastinating on a decision, especially the decision to "begin", absolves them of their responsibility to make that decision. The problem with this line of thinking is that not making a decision is in itself a decision! This type of thinking always leads to procrastination.

As you think about procrastination, don't beat yourself up about it. We all do this from time to time. The point is … how can we be better?

Exercise: *Think about the 3 basic categories of procrastinators. Which do you usually fall into when you procrastinate?*

DAY TWENTY-EIGHT
PROCRASTINATION

#3: **CONSEQUENCES** OF PROCRASTINATION

As we think about procrastination, it is valuable to assess its consequences. If we can see some of the damage that it does, we are probably better equipped to resist it or to turn it around when we do succumb to it.

So, let's consider what sorts of consequences it might have on our lives. Typically, delaying the performance of some assignments or tasks can lead to traumatic situations. I can think of many things that procrastination has cost me over the years. There are times when it has brought failure to my life: failure to complete a task or an assignment, or failure to do that task well because of the time constraints. There are times when it has cost me money; there are times when it has cost me reputation in the eyes of other people. There are times when it has damaged relationships, because people were counting on me, and my procrastination let them down.

Sometimes it leads to the loss of a job or a title or an honor. Sometimes it just leads to the loss of respect – both from others and for ourselves. Procrastination ultimately leads to lower self-esteem. We all seem to know deep inside when we are procrastinating. Oh, we kid ourselves, we cover it up, but we still know. When we know we have not done what we are capable of doing, and we have put off those things that were necessary, and we have acted in a way that was detrimental to our own best interest … we begin to lose respect for ourselves.

When self-esteem begins to suffer, so many other areas sustain losses as well. There have been times when I have felt weak and useless and helpless because of procrastination. It creates a high degree of dissatisfaction and frustration, not only among other people, but internally as well. Procrastination can then lead to physical consequences. As the weight of guilt, stress, and fear takes its toll, experts tell us that it can greatly affect our health. We may lose sleep, and our immune systems may even be compromised.[7]

I think we can agree together that the consequences that come as a result of procrastination are serious and undesirable and that there must be a better way.

Exercise: *Do you see these consequences manifesting in your life when you procrastinate? Which consequences do you feel the effects of most?*

DAY TWENTY-NINE
PROCRASTINATION

#4: **RECOGNIZING** PROCRASTINATION

As we've discussed before, the biggest part of defeating procrastination in our lives is simply recognizing it! Today we are going to talk about some warning signs that can let us know that we are procrastinating. Now, it's almost always easier to see these warning signs in others than it is to see them in ourselves. But here is our goal for today: to be totally open and honest about these warning signs. Let's all consider today whether or not any of them are true in our own lives and, if they are, let's move towards doing something about it.

Warning sign #1: *Low self-confidence*
These procrastinators frequently think: "I'm not good enough. I'm inadequate. I can't keep up. I have (x) problem that makes me less than a normal person."

Warning sign #2: *Chronic busyness*
These procrastinators frequently think: "I'm too busy. My schedule is too full. My affairs are complicated and demanding and I have no choice but to put this off."

Warning sign #3: *Stubbornness and pride*
These procrastinators frequently think: "Don't tell me when to do something, I'll do it when I'm good and ready. Don't tell me what's good for me, I've got myself figured out.

Warning sign #4: *Manipulation*
These procrastinators frequently think: "If I don't do my part, then you can't do your part, and I'll have the power in this relationship." (Sometimes the thought process here isn't so calculated or devious but the results are the same even when the thoughts are not clearly defined in this way.)

Warning sign #5: *Coping with pressure/stress*
These procrastinators frequently think: "I'm the victim here. No one should have to try and do (x) task while dealing with my situation. I'm stressed and tired and these problems I have are not my fault. I just have to give myself a break."

Warning sign #6: *Habitual procrastination*
These procrastinators frequently think: "This is just the way I am … I'll be better when the adrenaline rush hits. Procrastination is not a *problem* for me, it's just who I am."

Warning sign #7: *Distraction*
These procrastinators frequently think: "I can still get everything done, I just need to do this first. Oh look at that, I better do that next. You need me to handle something? Sure, I'll do that first. Oh I forgot about this. I'll have to take care of this before I can get to that other thing."

Exercise: *Which of these warning signs can you see in your life? After reading these, what task stands out to you right now as something you are procrastinating on?*

DAY THIRTY
PROCRASTINATION

#5: **AVOIDING** PROCRASTINATION

All right! It's time to wrap up this study on procrastination so we can get out there and stop procrastinating! It's time to execute some plans, begin some tasks, and achieve some goals. Here are some ways to handle the temptation to procrastinate.

Step #1: *Do what is most important*
Here is the severe interpretation that I have had to take in order for me to begin to gain on the challenge of procrastination in my life. *Anything that comes in the way of the most important thing to do right now is procrastination.* Resist the urge to handle the urgent rather than the important. Handle the important.

Step #2: *Establish your priorities*
Make a list of your priorities in life, and then rank your to-do list accordingly. Don't allow the pressure of others' disproval or judgment upon your priorities to cause you to feel guilt about sticking to them. And don't allow yourself to be pulled away from those priorities because of urgencies that crop up.

Step #3: *Evaluate the excuses*
Assess the interior monologue in your head when it comes to something you think you might be procrastinating on. If anything sounds like some of the interior thoughts of the 7 warning signs from yesterday, you may want to make some deliberate choices to look at the task from a better perspective.

Step #4: *Find an accountability partner*
Find someone who is as committed to abolishing procrastination in his or her life as you are in your own. Determine to track your productive hours each day for a week, in half-hour intervals. Then come together and assess your productivity. The accountability will produce extremely favorable results. Be sure that your partner does not validate your excuses … they are there to help you win, not to make you feel good.

Step #5: *Be honest in your self-evaluation*
It is true that there are times when you need to rest, or to put dreams and goals on the back burner for the sake of some other season in life. It is true that occasionally you might be too stressed or overloaded. However, be sure that you are not validating things that are not true. You know yourself, your capacity, your priorities. Determine those things and then hold yourself to them. No one else can do it for you.

Exercise: *Let's get started with step #1. What is one important thing you can do in the next 30 minutes? Write it down and then GO DO IT! Watch how it influences your self-esteem for the better.*

DAY THIRTY-ONE
HUMILITY

Based on my experience of life and knowledge of people, I have come to believe that many people tend to misunderstand what true humility really is. Here's what I believe it to be: a quiet acknowledgment of, and an *appreciation* for, the gifts and strengths that we possess.

Now, that may or may not be your definition of humility. Many people think that humility has more to do with self-deprecation, with belittling our strengths and not taking credit where credit is genuinely due. By many standards, a humble person is one who doesn't appreciate his own gifts, but rather seeks to demean them.

The longer I live, the more convinced I become that a proper understanding of what being humble is all about must involve *positive* attention to one's gifts.

Gifts are not something to demean or hide or discredit.

In fact, psychologists and teachers and coaches and leaders all agree, the vast majority of greatness comes from focusing on our strengths. This focus is not in a way that belittles others; it's a confident acceptance that our strengths and our gifts are exactly that: *gifts*.

If we truly believe that they are gifts, then that would eliminate all boasting about who we are and what we do. Pride would be replaced with a thankful acknowledgement of a gift and that gratitude would lead to an acceptance of a responsibility to use our gifts.

If we are not grateful for the gifts that we have, we are likely to become bitter over what we don't have. Bitterness is a poor substitute for humility. There is nothing that connects those two together in a meaningful way. But if we can focus our attention upon the gifts that we have been given, we will avoid bitterness over our perceived shortcomings.

Our humility also voids a need for the one-upmanship that so frequently poisons relationships. If we could somehow eliminate that kind of comparative, competitive culture, it would be a different world. Of course, we cannot change the culture of the world in which we live, and most people adjust to living within a framework of comparison and competition. Here's a thought, though: we can change ourselves, and thereby influence the atmosphere of the world in which we live.

So that's why we commit to personal development. That's why we commit to *Daily Disciplines*. When we consistently remind ourselves that we have gifts that are worth appreciating and exploring, we choose to exit that comparative, competitive framework. Instead, we discover that we can exist in something so much more inspiring and motivating: a place where we embrace our gifts and work each day towards becoming all that we are created to be.

Exercise: *What are some of your "gifts"? What is one way that you have shown gratitude this week for one of your gifts?*

DAY THIRTY-TWO
DELEGATION

My perfectionistic nature has created a lot of challenges over the course of my life. The importance of delegation was a really tough lesson for me to learn. Somehow, I used to have the idea that admitting I needed help on a project was somehow acknowledging a weakness. Once I overcame this faulty perspective, the benefits I enjoyed were substantial.

Let me take a moment to explore why this was such a sticking point for me. When I set out to accomplish something, I want that task to be done with excellence. Years ago when I went to do something, it had to be *perfect*. There is a great difference between excellence and perfection. When I was a youngster mowing lawns, I would trim the edges with hand clippers because it just looked better. I gave top-quality manicures to those yards. So when I started to become familiar with the idea of delegation, it was very difficult for me to accept. How could I know that the job others would do would be as good as mine? The effort that I perceived it would take to "fix" their mistakes seemed like more of a burden to me than simply doing it all myself.

Well, I suppose that sounds a little prideful, doesn't it? But the fact is, some personalities just have that perfectionistic nature. And that's okay … it can be honed into a pursuit of excellence. Over time I came to the point where I realized that to accomplish certain things, I had to have a team of people and I had to trust that they would do an excellent job. As I began to accept this truth, I had another breakthrough. I attended a seminar by John Maxwell and he made some comments that were profound to me. To summarize, he had concluded that he was good at *only four things*, and if the task required something outside of those four things, he needed to find someone else to do it. He went on to add that they would do the task far better than he could have done it, and collectively they would accomplish things on a much larger scale with greater impact and a higher degree of excellence.[8]

I still believe that we are equipped to do anything we set our minds to do so long as we can conceive and believe it. The realization I came to is that just because we *can*, doesn't mean we *should*.

We will learn more on another day about our gifts, talents, and areas of expertise. For now, let's focus on empowering others and trusting them to accomplish their parts of the task with excellence. This requires us to select the correct people for the job we are delegating, and that can be a learning process – but it's one worth pursuing. When we learn to see and encourage and empower the talents and gifts of others, we discover a whole new way of achieving excellence together.

Exercise: *What is a project that you are currently working on that could benefit from the use of effective delegation? How can you implement this?*

DAY THIRTY-THREE
WHAT AM I GREAT AT?

PART **ONE**

During my early days of study, as I began to search for a better way to live, I devoted a lot of time to researching all that human beings are capable of. I discovered irrefutable evidence that we as humans have an amazing potential that goes largely untapped. I became convinced that there is so much more that we are capable of, and part of my studies turned to determining how to take advantage of the amazing minds and bodies with which our Creator has blessed us.

Here's what I believe: you can do anything that you set your mind to do. When you come to believe that you are an incredible creation with vast potential, it is *powerful*. You can do anything that you *set your mind to do*. Now, this means that you probably cannot and will not do things that are beyond the realm of your current understanding of scientific possibilities – things like time travel or flying. What it means is that you can do what you truly *believe* you can do.

Today we are going to take this understanding a step further. I have also learned that the refining of this belief is extremely valuable. Just because "I can", doesn't mean "I should". This may be confusing. You may be saying, "But Skip, didn't you just say I could do *anything*?"

Yes. I did. However … I have come to learn that we each have unique areas that we are *gifted* in, and the more we focus on these areas, the more we can accomplish. Our task then becomes discovering the things that we are really good at and then focusing our attention and time and effort on those things. When we do, we will be amazed by our productivity, achievement, and satisfaction with our lives.

Here's my observation about our world today: there are lots of "cool" and worthwhile things. Change and technology are accelerating. We learn more, and we learn it at a faster pace. The sheer volume of possibilities in our world can create a distraction trap that can impede us from fully discovering our *own* gifts and passions and strengths. We can try lots of things, and we should, so that we can discover what we like. But if we try to become *good* at everything, then we will probably miss out on being *great* at a few things.

The first thing we can conclude, then, is that there are lots of interests, careers, and life paths that we could choose, and each of them offers rewards. The second thing we can conclude is that *we are not meant to go down all of those paths*. So let's focus our thoughts today on what we truly believe we are created to do and to become.

Exercise: *What do you believe that you are created to become? What are you currently doing that might be a distraction to that purpose?*

DAY THIRTY-FOUR
WHAT AM I GREAT AT?

PART **TWO**

There are many factors that can make it difficult to determine what it is that you are really good at—what it is that you are created to do. Sometimes, there is pressure from family to pursue a certain path. Sometimes, that pressure or influence can come from others that you respect or admire – you work towards the things that they encourage you to work towards because you want to please and impress them. Other times, you may go down a path because it seems noble or sacrificial and you feel obligated to share your portion of the load. Sadly, all of these are the wrong reasons and will lead you to restlessness and discontentment when you find yourself far along a path that you never should have taken in the first place.

So how do you find the path that you *should* follow?

This is not an easy question. Maybe the place to start is to ask yourself what you *like* to do. If you aren't sure of the answer to this, you may want to go try out a few things that you think you might like. Doing this will require the investment of time and it will require you to embrace the risks associated with stepping outside your comfort zone. These risks are well worth taking, however, if they lead you to the discovery of your passions and strengths.

Another option is to seek out input from mentors in your life. This may be your parents, spouse, professors, professional colleagues, or close friends. This input can be really helpful. I do need to advise you to be very careful to choose your mentors wisely. You are opening yourself up to receive direct input on the future of your life, and the possibility of unwise or even harmful input is an ever-present reality. Or you may take their advice and find yourself on a path of trying to please or impress them, which is what you are trying to avoid. You may also get general discouragement if you choose someone who has stopped dreaming for his own life.

A third method to discover what you are really good at is to do a sort of self-inventory. You could create your own, and begin by listing things that you like doing and areas that bring you satisfaction. What talents have you discovered? There are also many books and tests that can help you through this process and help you to understand yourself better. I do add that you should be careful not to let a book or test typecast you. Even the best assessments out there can make some people feel categorized instead of empowered. These guides can give you some great insights, but remember that they are general, and you are still unique.

Here's what I would recommend: ask the mentors of your life for input and use the guides to learn more about yourself. Process both of these things and use them to reduce your options. Then start trying out the best options! You might just discover what it is that you are great at doing.

The rewards of this process are vast. Understanding your talents and being able to apply them will bring great joy into your life. It will also allow you to find others who have complementary talents and together I believe you will accomplish wonderful things.

Exercise: *What are some things that you would like to try out as a part of this process?*

DAY THIRTY-FIVE
FALLING SHORT

If I'm really honest with myself, I don't particularly enjoy our topic for today.

In my early years, I wouldn't have talked about this at all. I wanted to be perfect. I thought in terms of perfection and aimed for perfection, and so whenever I fell short of that perfection, it was a disastrous experience. If that sounds like you, then be encouraged. I grew out of my perfectionism, and you can too.

Although I am now older and wiser and a little easier on myself, I still don't specifically like to take a close look at the areas in my life where I have fallen short. I would prefer to measure my success, to see the areas in my life where I am improving! And there is certainly value in tracking accomplishment and focusing on positive change.

But there is also value in taking some time every once in a while to evaluate the places where I have fallen short. There can be a positive purpose in looking at relationships that I didn't invest enough time in, or areas of my life where I am lacking discipline, or goals that I failed to achieve. The fact is that failure is always going to be a part of the growth process; therefore, if I am seeking to grow, I am also accepting the fact that I will fail.

The question is … what do we do with the failures and disappointments and shortcomings? Do we beat ourselves up about them? Do we replay them over and over in our minds, proving to ourselves that failure is our only possible outcome? Do we use them as evidence that we should abandon ship on our dreams and hopes for becoming what we are created to be?

I certainly hope not! That would be a very foolish way to spend our mental time, and that is certainly not what I am suggesting that any of us do.

Instead of viewing our shortcomings through a negative perspective, let's choose to have an attitude of excitement and anticipation. Let's acknowledge that these realizations of our shortcomings can be a great benefit to us in moving forward. They can reveal to us that perhaps we need to change some priorities or look into finding a different vehicle to reach our dream. They can expose areas where we need to focus on more discipline and areas where we need to apply a little more grace.

When we accept the fact that falling short is going to be part of the process in becoming all we are created to be, we can find it's benefit and choose to learn from it, every time.

Exercise: *Write down some areas where you feel you've fallen short. Remember that it's okay to not be perfect.*

DAY THIRTY-SIX
WHY DAILY?

Today is a simple reminder that our focus needs to be on a daily commitment to personal growth. Over the years, I have discovered that even with a career that focuses on teaching personal growth to others, I still need reminders of how it affects me if I forget to focus on the day-to-day discipline of it all. That is the very purpose of this book – to provide us with a quick and simple way to engage this type of thinking every day.

But let's think a little deeper about why that is so important, and about how we can encourage ourselves to continue the daily process of discovering and becoming all that we are created to be.

Those who get really good at focusing every day on little things will soon discover that they can do more and then more. Now, one would think, one would hope, that this becomes more instinctual after a while. But I have learned that it doesn't take much distraction to pull us away from our well-formed habits … and it also seems to take a large amount of effort to pick those habits back up again.

So what helps us stay committed?

For me, it's reminders. Reminders that each and every day there is something I can change for the better. In my thinking, my actions, or my conversations, I need to do something every day. This understanding is truly one of the great secrets of life.

So today and every day, let's be deliberate. Let's purposefully choose to engage study and thought, whether we feel like it or not. Let's persistently choose to do the simple exercises provided in this book, whether it seems like we have time for them or not. Let's steadfastly commit to being in control of our interior monologue and to encouraging our own self-talk towards the positive and uplifting side of the spectrum. Let's tirelessly pursue the idea that we can indeed become all that we are created to be.

Exercise: Evaluate your daily routine. Where is one place you can be more deliberate about personal growth?

DAY THIRTY-SEVEN |
TEACHABILITY |

During the summer when we have training with the staff at Circle A, we often invest a good amount of time talking about the subject of teachability. My hope is that each member of the leadership team will be open to learning more and that they will discover that whatever stage of life they come to, they *always* have something to learn.

What is teachability? It boils down to being willing to learn.

You have to be willing to learn. I know this seems simple, but it's often amazing to me how unwilling people really are to learn. Employers continue to find recent graduates *and* experienced employees that are set in the ways they do things. They think they know the best way and aren't receptive to the training that their new employer offers. For these employers, it means a large investment of money into hiring and training new employees, only to have to repeat this process at additional cost because the people they have hired are not teachable.

On the surface, most of us probably believe that we are teachable. Yet when we are presented with opportunities to learn, we frequently dismiss them because we believe we already know how to handle things. This isn't to say that we should just take everything we are told without analyzing it and comparing it to our experience, value structure, and training. What I am suggesting is that we need to be constantly in the process of *seeking knowledge, wisdom, and common sense*. We must accept that while we may know a lot, there is always more to know. We can always improve. And even if what we are being taught is not the best way to do something, we can always pull some lesson out of every experience that is of benefit to us.

We also need to keep our hearts and minds open to learning when we hear something that rubs us the wrong way or that is in opposition to our way of thinking. We don't have to accept what is being said as truth, but we can hear all of it before we decide what we can take away from the material for our benefit.

I'm again brought back to how essential this skill is to success in all areas of life. I would encourage you to keep it in mind the next time you are being presented with material, either at work, your place of worship, or just reading an article. Having the attitude that everyone has something to teach me and that I always have something to learn is a great mindset in life!

Exercise: *Is there a place or a person in your life that creates an atmosphere in which you have decided that it is okay for you to be resistant to learning? Why is that? Can you think of a way to still choose to be teachable?*

DAY THIRTY-EIGHT
TOUGH QUESTIONS

I've found over the years that questions are capable—when answered honestly—of revealing truths that are incredibly valuable to our life's journey. I've been told by people I've coached over the years that I have a knack for asking tough questions that really cause them to stop, evaluate where they are at, and then clearly discover a path to continue on. I can assure you that asking questions like this didn't come naturally and is something that has developed over time. And I can assure you that asking these questions does little good if we are not willing to stop, assess, and give a really honest answer.

During our time today we are going to be thinking about questions that we ask ourselves. While some of these questions can be really tough for us to answer, they are key to staying on the path to real success and being committed to a process of self-discovery.

Whenever I am faced with a challenge or new experience or even a great victory, I like to ask questions that cause me to truly reflect upon where I am and how I got there—questions like: *What is good in this situation? What can I learn from this? How did I arrive in this situation? What is my body language saying right now? Why do I feel afraid? Why do I feel happy? or Is this leading me towards becoming the person that I am created to be?*

Another really important part of developing the skill of asking yourself questions is to learn how to ask follow-up questions. If you try a new food, it isn't enough to simply ask yourself, "Do I like this?" The follow-up question would be, "Why do I like this?" Do you like the food because it actually tastes good? Or do you like it because you are eating with a friend and the friend really, really wants you to like the food? Or do you like it because of the beautiful presentation and surroundings while you are eating it?

I think you can understand the process here. The purpose of these questions—in the food analogy but more importantly in the greater growth opportunities of life—is to be self-aware. When we discover how to ask ourselves not only about our assessment of things, but also our reasons for that assessment, we are on a path to self-discovery that will certainly help us make better choices and learn more from each experience that we have along the way. I have one word of warning in this process: be fair to yourself. Honesty does not equate to debilitating self-criticism. Ask yourself the tough questions, give yourself the honest answers, and then be kind to yourself as you process those answers and move forward towards becoming all that you are created to be.

Exercise: *What is one experience or problem that you need to ask yourself some tough questions about? What are the tough questions?*

DAY THIRTY-NINE
ACCOUNTABILITY

We thought yesterday about some of the tough questions we ask ourselves. One area that I cautioned on was being too hard or overly critical of ourselves with the answers. Today, we will look at a solution for that: having an accountability partner or a mentor.

What I'm suggesting is that we seek out and cultivate a healthy relationship with someone who is on the path of becoming the best version of himself. When a relationship like that is safe and commensurate and both parties agree to hold each other accountable for the process of personal growth, huge advancement can be made.

For some of us, this person may be our spouse. They can tell us if we are being too hard or too easy-going with our responses to self-evaluation questions. However, having this relationship with our spouse isn't always a good idea because sometimes it is very tempting to be overly critical of a spouse. You can both *want* to give each other healthy feedback—and you can even *want* to receive that feedback—but sometimes it does not work in the dynamic of the relationship. If it works for you and your spouse, great! If not, I'd prefer to say, "make it work!" But I recognize the resistance that some have to this idea. So take heart – there are other options.

There may be a friend or partner or teammate who could be this accountability partner for you. As you cultivate this relationship with your accountability partner, keep in mind that you will also have the opportunity to hold him accountable and to ask tough questions. Tread lightly here. Remember that your input can profoundly affect his life. Do your very best to leave your accountability partner better than you found him.

Sometimes there is not a readily apparent accountability partner in our lives. In that case, we may need to find a life coach or a counselor. This would be someone who helps to keep you accountable and gives you an external perspective. In most cases, this person has a rate she charges for providing these services. Sometimes, a pastor or mentor or leader in your life could fill this role without receiving compensation for her counseling. All of these people may, given their external view, be able to ask a tough question that cuts through all of the layers of your perspective right to the heart of the problem.

As valuable as this is, I'm always cautious when finding mentors or accountability partners in my life. When I am truly transparent with a person, I am vulnerable. If I choose a mentor poorly, he could quite easily do me severe harm, even if he has good intentions. My good friend Nancy Dornan frequently says, "Remember, every person is a package." Every person has his own weaknesses and perspectives and insecurities. We are all human, and so we are all flawed. Keeping that in mind, it is certainly possible for you to find a person who is aligned with your beliefs about life and about personal development. As long as you don't set this person up to be the one who defines you and gives you the answers to all of your problems, an accountability relationship can be extremely beneficial.

The path to becoming our best selves is one that is lined with safe, healthy, life-giving relationships. It is not a path we are meant to walk alone.

Exercise: *What person or people in your life are potential accountability partners or mentors? Are you willing to pursue an accountability relationship with them?*

For the past 40+ years of teaching *Dynamic Living*, I have always taught that there are 10 principles of success. Recently, I began to teach principles number 11 and 12 in the *Dynamic Living* seminar at our Circle A summer camp. It is not that I just discovered them after all these years, but rather that I have become confident enough in my understanding of them and in my being able to live with them, that I can now talk to others about them. Personal integrity is one of those principles.

Integrity, according to my personal definition, means being consistent or congruent on the inside and the outside of one's life.

Integrity is all about saying what you mean and meaning what you say. There was a time in our history when all one had to do was say it and you could count on it. The phrase, "my word is my bond," came from those times. Later, integrity was symbolized by a handshake. As we have digressed more and more from an integrous way of living, our society now makes statements more like, "That contract is not even worth the paper it is written on." There is little integrity in business practices and in many relationships. Our guiding system as a culture is based more on what can be proven right or wrong in a court of law rather than on a simple custom of integrity.

Here's how I like to think of it: inside, outside, upside, downside – all the same, all the time.

Well … that can sound rather impossible sometimes, can't it? That can sound like we have to attain a standard of perfection in order to have integrity. You may be saying, "Skip, I'm not sure I've got a good handle on what you mean by personal integrity. It sounds as though you are talking about perfection! I'm not sure I'm capable of that!"

Oh, how well I know that struggle. But I have come to understand that perfection is not required in order to be a person of integrity nor to achieve significance in life. The pursuit of excellence is what I am personally after. When we recognize that perfection in the human experience is not possible, and when we come to the humble realization that there is a necessity for a *lifetime* of personal growth, we then will have a livable and rewarding combination of ingredients for our goal. To approach life with the arrogance that says "I am perfect" is a quintessential expression of a *lack* of integrity. And so, it is not about perfection. It is about a relentless *pursuit* of integrity: deliberately making the choice to be the same on the inside as we are on the outside.

A life of integrity will be one of the most rewarding, successful, significant, impacting lives that you can imagine. Let's all work towards this life together.

Exercise: *What is one place in your life where you observe a lack of integrity? Is it in word, thought, or deed? What is a way that you can begin to strengthen your integrity in that area?*

DAY FORTY-ONE |
LOOK FOR THE GOOD |

During our summer camp program, we invest some time at the beginning of the session to go over the guidelines that will help us create the environment that is Circle A. One of these guidelines is that we all commit to look for the good in others and then to talk about it. This is a vital part of creating the atmosphere because it helps us get out of the world of competitive comparison. This allows us to build each other up instead of tear each other down. For some, looking for the good in others comes quite naturally. Susan is a great encourager and it just flows out of her. For others of us, this is something we have to work on.

Now, the intention behind this has to be right and free of any agenda. Compliments that build others up are only meaningful if they are genuinely given. If I give a compliment to you with the expectation that you will say something kind to me in return, it negates the compliment. Or, if I give a compliment to you that is clearly untrue and disingenuous, it feels like a put-down. It feels like a sarcastic comment that is intended to make fun of you, rather than my deliberate effort to look for something good.

Here's what I've discovered: there is good to find in every person, in every circumstance, in every day, and in every life. The more we look for the good, the more we discover that there really is good to find.

Another guideline we discuss at Circle A is leaving a place better than we found it. For just a minute, let's think about applying this to people. How much different would our world be if we tried to leave everyone we meet better than we found them? This concept goes a little deeper than merely paying compliments. If I'm encountering others and trying to learn about them, and if I'm investing myself in talking about all the good things I'm seeing in them—without expecting anything specific in return—both my life and their lives will be made better.

Can I be real honest with you? Since you've read this far, I'm taking that as a yes. When I'm thinking about this area, there's really a deeper truth that is worth exploring.

I have come to learn that one of the great joys of life is relating to others and seeing their different perspectives and all the wonders of their experiences. I'm often overwhelmed by the rich and beautiful tapestry of people that are in my life. While it is important and helpful for me to invest time in self-reflection, I can't allow myself to stay closed off from the depth of life experiences that can be found in a community of people. As an introvert, it would be easier for me to stay secluded – but there is so much more to life when we learn to truly see and celebrate the good in every person we meet.

Exercise: *Who in your life can you deliberately focus on seeing the good in? Write down their names and begin to look for and speak about the good things you see in those people.*

DAY FORTY-TWO |
URGENCY |

We have already discussed the principle of action and the motto, DO IT NOW! This is a short and powerful principle, and we have learned the impact of decisive and deliberate action. Today we will visit an idea that goes hand-in-hand with action: urgency.

You may be thinking to yourself, "Skip, that's really the same thing." Initially I would probably have agreed with you. However, the more I thought about it, the more it became clear that there is a distinction that should be made. While action is always important, I think urgency applies more to the *attitude* of the action.

Let me give you an example. A friend of mine is studying martial arts, and there is a particular routine he has to learn and master before he can move on to the next level. He went over it with his instructor, and they determined that in order to master the move, he needed to run through it one hundred times. So he then had a choice. He could decide to run through the move once a week until he had done it one hundred times, or he could decide to run through it 20 times a day and master it quickly. Both of these are plans that involve taking deliberate action, but the second one is with a sense of urgency.

Urgency is taking action with an awareness of purpose. When I focus on walking, I walk fast. Anyone observing me walking knows that I am going someplace with purpose. I can recall many trips to Disney World when the kids were little where I would set the pace for the family's speed of movement. It was fast. The kids sometimes had to run to keep up, but they were always intrigued by the way that people would naturally part for us because of our pace and sense of urgency. I'm quite certain we covered twice the ground of an average family at Disney!

Even at Circle A, I often walk quickly when I am going from one place on campus to another. This sets an example for our leadership team and our campers that we are not just going through the motions; we are *taking action with a purpose*. I want to communicate this sense of urgency through my body language. I am moving with purpose, I'm focused and there is no time to waste because my goal is important to me.

Now, we have to temper the sense of urgency so that it doesn't turn into an unhealthy pressure or haste that will lead to mistakes and burnout. Rushing our goals or our teams or ourselves is usually ineffective. Remember, a sense of urgency is less about the *speed* it takes to accomplish the action, and more about a confident, deliberate, enthusiastic *attitude* about taking the action.

Action is vital when we are working to accomplish our goals. Urgency is the multiplying power of the action that will increase our pace and let us cross the finish line sooner.

Exercise: *Do you have a plan of action that could be enhanced with a sense of urgency? What would that look like?*

DAY FORTY-THREE
AN HONEST LOOK

Yesterday is gone, but it would be a major mistake to assume that it is, *or should be*, forgotten. Though yesterday has passed, it is still a part of today, and it will always be a part of every tomorrow.

Sometimes as we travel down the path of becoming all we are created to be, it is beneficial to pause and take a look at our past. Our past holds all sorts of truths and revelations and lessons that sometimes we overlook in the moment, and only can truly grasp them when we look at these things from a distance.

There are interactions, experiences, and times of both great difficulty and great joy that can unlock pieces of wisdom, maturity, and strength within us; but in order to access these benefits, we have to take an honest look at the past. We also must always remember that looking into our past is never for the purpose of assigning guilt or blame or shame; it is never meant for camping out amidst our mistakes and regrets and losing sight of our present or future. A look at the past should never be about the opinions of others and it should never get us stuck in a web of over-analyzing that we cannot easily escape from.

A healthy look at the past starts with one thing: honesty. So often, when we begin to look at the past, we become defensive. We try to justify our actions to ourselves or to whomever we feel like we need to convince. If we are going to learn from our experiences, then we have to drop the rationalizing. We have to stop making excuses and assigning blame and we need to embrace the phrase that I repeat so often to myself: I am responsible.

Our past can create healthy, powerful, insightful building blocks for our future, if we choose to look back with honesty.

Exercise: Think about a time in your past when you felt defensive? What were you trying to justify in that situation? Write down an honest account of what happened and then decide what you can learn from it.

DAY FORTY-FOUR
AFFIRMATIONS REVISITED

Have you begun work on your affirmations yet? I find that although I write and speak about affirmations constantly, most people merely think about the idea and never actually get around to doing it. Have you? Maybe you were able to get a couple down, but then you stopped because you became distracted or perhaps you couldn't think of anything else to write.

The reality is that we can affirm most anything that we want to be true in our lives. We can affirm things that we want to accomplish or things about the type of people we want to be. I fully believe that when we commit to writing and reading our affirmations on a regular basis, we will make positive, lasting change in our lives. That's what I want for you. This little step of writing down affirmations can have a powerful, life-altering effect on you!

Here's a list of some other affirmations that I have used about myself to give you some inspiration and a place to start.

I have a positive expectancy of the future because I know I'm accomplishing my goals.

I have pride in my performance.

I look for ways to lift people up.

I have a great emotional sense of connection with the people in my life.

I am a happy person.

I have a quiet, emotional, magnetic strength when I speak.

As we affirm these kinds of things about ourselves, I believe we will discover that our lives will begin changing and that we will become more and more like the people we desire to be. You can do this—you deserve the effort that it will take.

Today I challenge you to make a list of some affirmations about you as a person, about your goals in life, about the things you'd like to have happen to you. Then begin the process of affirming them on a daily basis.

Exercise: *Write an affirmation here that specifically references an attribute of the type of person you would like to be.*

DAY FORTY-FIVE
THE CRITIC WITHIN

We talked before about critics and their good intentions, and we also discussed some ways to handle the critics. Let's take it a step further today. Here is a thought: sometimes the toughest critic is the one within.

This critic can be the harshest of all, and yet often I don't even realize the havoc he is wreaking on my life. *Wreaking.* Is that a good word?

When we set out to accomplish our dream, we make goals and determine the disciplines we need to form in order to have a successful journey. We coach ourselves along the way and we often critique our actions, observing what we did wrong and hopefully encouraging what we did right.

Sometimes in this process, the inner voice becomes a drill sergeant of sorts. If we are not careful, we can become a negative voice to ourselves, dishing out criticism instead of positive reinforcement.

The problem we often face is that the drill sergeant takes over and we lose sight of all we are doing right. It is not helpful nor healthy to merely beat ourselves up for everything we are doing wrong. Some may call this self-discipline, but that's not what it is. It's self-abuse. It leads down an unhealthy path that will soon have us lashing out at others because we stop feeling good about ourselves. If we are fixated on our mistakes and failures, we can become paralyzed by our own criticism.

The key here is a perspective shift: we must work to turn the inner critic into the inner coach. Does this mean we won't make mistakes? Or that we will simply ignore errors all together? No. Of course we will fall short. But our inner coach reminds us to learn from the failure, to see how we could have done it differently, and then to focus on doing better the next time. Finally, our inner coach reminds us to be grateful for a stepping-stone to a better future.

Just as we learned about giving grace to our critics and understanding that their intentions are usually good, let's choose to give grace to ourselves too in those times when the inner coach turns into the inner critic. Let's remember that a consistent pattern of engaging positive thoughts and ideas will strengthen our inner coach and silence our inner critic. Here's the good news: they have separate volume controls … and we have sole possession of the dials.

Exercise: Are you beating yourself up inside in the name of self-discipline? What's one area of your life where you can take control of the inner critic?

DAY FORTY-SIX
SUPERHIGHWAYS TO THE LAND OF YOUR NIGHTMARES #1

I suppose the title of this day might startle you – it certainly feels strange to me to write it! But sometimes, there is a benefit to shock value because it forces our minds to process things just a little bit differently. So, for the next 6 days, we are going to engage in some alternative, uncomfortable thinking. My hope is that we can discover some paths that, when followed, will unquestionably take us towards defeat and sorrow. This discovery will empower us to *stay away* from those highways. We can learn the road signs so that we can get off the highway if we are on one, and then we will find a better road to travel together.

So, let's begin.

The first superhighway to the land of your nightmares is the "Feelings First Freeway". This is a dangerous and destructive road, on which the traveler decides that his feelings come first. The traveler makes decisions based on what helps him to *feel good* or what helps him avoid feeling bad. The traveler stops reasoning and ceases to look ahead for the consequences of his actions. He moves forward on the basis of trying to simply feel good in the moment. When a situation arises that doesn't offer an opportunity to feel good, his decisions will be based on avoiding that situation entirely.

The traveler on the "Feelings First Freeway" resists all efforts to think deliberately about the positive aspects of life. When faced with a challenge or pain, this person will resist the idea of trying to find the good in the situation or will refuse to acknowledge the growth opportunities. He may lash out, trying to inflict pain on someone else in an ineffective attempt to make himself feel better. His thoughts will be controlled by his feelings – when he feels pressured or cheated or angered, he will allow his mind to dwell on it. When he feels good or encouraged or happy, he will allow his mind to dwell on it. Feelings dictate thinking on the "Feelings First Freeway". Internal personal integrity is compromised and violated on an increasingly frequent schedule.

This superhighway is more of a rollercoaster, traversing countless ups and downs and corkscrews and free falls on its way to an unfulfilled and disappointing ending. The traveler on this highway will miss countless lessons and chances for joy because he is too bogged down with his own feelings. He will start to be disillusioned with the high points on the road because he knows another low point is just around the bend. He will keep searching for the next mountaintop experience, only to keep finding himself in the next valley that follows. Eventually, he will not even recognize the positive experiences that do come along and will see almost every situation through a lens of negativity.

Is this happening to you in some form? I have an affirmation that I mentioned in an earlier segment that addresses this: "My actions are based on what I know I should be doing and not on my emotions. My emotions are ever-changing." This affirmation works for avoiding Superhighway #1, and can help you get off it should you find yourself already on it.

Exercise: Have you ever found yourself on the "Feelings First Freeway"? Are you on it now? If so, recognize where, and write down one positive thing about the situation. Choose today to let your mind focus on the positive thing you have written.

DAY FORTY-SEVEN
SUPERHIGHWAYS TO THE LAND OF YOUR NIGHTMARES #2

The second superhighway that will take us straight to a land of nightmares is the "Uncontrolled Access Throughway". The traveler on the "Uncontrolled Access Throughway" believes that the process of prioritizing her life and establishing goals is a waste of time and not really worth the effort. She has no differentiation of priorities for items on her agenda; anything can be allowed on her to-do list at any time.

There is no deliberate direction on this highway; travelers are blown whichever way the winds of obligation and circumstance and opinion take them. While those that find themselves living this way may be momentarily productive and successful, it is rarely fulfilling or sustainable.

Travelers on the "Uncontrolled Access Throughway" can sometimes feel very important and valued in the circles that they influence because they tend to be the ones who always say "yes", and who pile more on their plates than they are actually capable of handling with excellence and joy. They don't set boundaries and their identity is frequently based on a quest to please the people around them.

The traveler on this superhighway will find herself overwhelmed and exhausted, with no real direction in life. Her passions will be sacrificed or forgotten or never even fully discovered because she is too busy reacting to life rather than designing her life. She will also frequently have no deliberate barriers to negative influence from the people in her life and will be pulled down into pessimistic thinking and behavior because she allows everything to enter her mind unfiltered.

Feelings of "always being busy" yet "never accomplishing anything" are road signs that one might see on this highway. The inability to say "no" to things is another road sign. If a traveler does not know the exit number for her destination, it is another indication that she may be traveling this highway.

If at this point you are concerned that you are on this highway, you may want to ask yourself some questions. *Where am I headed? What is important to me? If I have two potential commitments and I can only do one, what determines my decision?* I would recommend asking these questions until you develop a hierarchy of priorities and a way to determine boundaries in your life. There is a section on priorities later in this book that will aid you in your thought process. Another series of questions might be: *Am I just pleasing people? Do I have a need for affirmation? Do I find my identity only in the value that I bring to others?*

There is only one way down this superhighway and it is never towards the land of your dreams. Unless you choose to turn off this highway and be deliberate with your life, your influences, and your direction, it will carry you directly towards your nightmares.

Exercise: *Have you ever found yourself on the "Uncontrolled Access Throughway"? Are you on it now? If so, recognize where. Now, write down one boundary that you can commit to today to start turning yourself off this path.*

DAY FORTY-EIGHT
SUPERHIGHWAYS TO THE LAND OF YOUR NIGHTMARES #3

The next superhighway to the land of your nightmares is the "Run-of-the-Mill Roundabout". This is less of a highway and more of a circular trap that keep its prisoners in a perpetual state of insignificance. The traveler of this particular road has decided that mediocrity is not only acceptable, but that it is the best state of being that he can hope to attain. Sometimes the traveler exits the "Feelings First Freeway" and gets on the "Run-of-the-Mill Roundabout". Avoidance of both pain and discomfort has become the driving force of his life.

On the "Run-of-the-Mill Roundabout", the prisoner caught within will set his expectations about life based on what he has been able to accomplish in the past and by observing what the vast majority of people do. He will accept that most people just don't amount to much and the best way to exist is to simply find a comfortable place and then never change or grow or aspire to be anything better. He may choose to associate with others stuck on the "Roundabout" because the atmosphere of similar thinking seems to validate his conclusion that mediocrity is a suitable state of being. He does just enough to get by, and finds things to do to simply pass time.

While the traveler on this superhighway might find a stretch of life where he is indeed able to simply "hang in there", there comes a time when his best attempts at comfort and mediocrity will fail him. Challenges in life take a great toll on these types of travelers because they have built their safety and comfort around the idea that nothing has to change. Therefore, job loss, sickness, death, friends leaving, or anything that shakes up the status quo becomes a very painful and catastrophic experience. Even good things, like the births of children, promotions, new opportunities, and new friends can be challenging and frequently uncomfortable.

These travelers will sometimes feel a pull to pursue a passion or dream, but they talk themselves out of it because they have accepted the lie that striving towards excellence and significance will bring a discomfort that is not worth the effort. They believe they are incapable of greatness and that seeking to discover the true nature of their worth will lead to disappointment.

And so they stay, imprisoned on the "Run-of-the-Mill Roundabout", working at avoiding anything that would cause pain, and refusing to pursue anything that would bring joy.

Road signs on the "Roundabout" are a little tricky, because the traveler will frequently see the same things again and again. This is a part of the trap. The traveler often takes comfort in things being familiar and so the fact that the road signs are the same isn't a cause for concern. But if you begin to see the same problems or challenges or feelings cropping up in your life throughout a variety of circumstances, you may want to give this superhighway a close look. There is a section about the comfort zone later in this book, and it will help you discover other ways of exiting the roundabout.

The questions for this highway are tough ones to ask. For most of us, this highway is a very easy place to find ourselves if we are not deliberately working to avoid it. While these questions are hard to ask myself, I have found that I need to ask them, lest I find myself the prisoner of the "Run-of-the-Mill-Roundabout". *When was the last time I had a different experience? When did I try something new or set a goal? Am I living life or just passing time?*

Exercise: *Have you ever found yourself trapped on the "Run-of-the-Mill Roundabout"? Are you on it now? Write down one change that would better your life if you decided to be brave enough to make that change.*

DAY FORTY-NINE
SUPERHIGHWAYS TO THE LAND OF YOUR NIGHTMARES #4

In the state of Kentucky there is a highway called the Bluegrass Parkway. It is a beautiful place to drive through the mountains and to take in the natural scenic landscapes that are dominant in that part of the country. On the Parkway, there are frequent pull-offs so that the driver and passengers can exit the car and take photographs or just gaze at the majesty of the surrounding mountains.

While this is a wonderful part of the Bluegrass Parkway, we need to be careful about traveling down a superhighway that has similar pull-off points. I call it the "Round-To-It Parkway" and it can be a dangerous place to travel.

A person driving down the "Round-To-It Parkway" will find her life filled with excuses. Whatever reasons and pull-off points she can come up with to stall her progress will turn into distractions and justifications as to why the goal is not being achieved. These distractions and excuses lead to procrastination, which can be a most deadly and vicious dream-killer.

Travelers of this superhighway are usually fixated on the idea that perfect conditions must arise before they can commence the journey towards their goal or dream or purpose. They want to be fully prepared and educated and informed and organized so that failure will not be an option. Their hearts are filled with a pressure towards perfection and if they do not feel that perfection can be attained, they will discover countless pull-off points to stop and assess or prepare or just plain *stall*.

Procrastination is deadly because the longer one procrastinates on a task or a dream or a goal, the harder it becomes to achieve. When excuses take over and distraction trumps conviction, it is difficult, if not impossible, to rekindle the passion and conviction once again. The longer a person lives in a state of making and accepting excuses, the easier those excuses are to find and validate. If you struggle with this superhighway, you may want to refer back to the section about procrastination earlier in this book.

The road signs on this superhighway are all about the roadside attractions. What is the next shiny object that I need to stop and observe? A traveller of this road might feel like she is driving a lot of miles but not ever reaching a destination. In other words, instead of getting much accomplished in life, she might just have a lot of experiences. Before long, she will find herself complacently parked on the side of a mountain, staring over at the land of her dreams, instead of getting in the car and driving there. And she will think the thought that has been heard and accepted by far too many: "Some day I'll go there … when I get around to it."

Exercise: *Have you ever found yourself trapped on the "Round-To-It-Parkway"? Are you on it now? Write down one thing you have been procrastinating on that you can take action on today.*

DAY FIFTY
SUPERHIGHWAYS TO THE LAND OF YOUR NIGHTMARES #5

If you have been around my teachings for very long, you have probably heard me talk about this superhighway before. I call it the "Poor-Little-Old-Me Turnpike". On this road, the traveler will buy into the lie that happiness comes to the lucky ones and that he is just not lucky. He will believe that some people just got a better break in life than he did and that it is simply his lot in life to suffer.

Travelers on the "Poor-Little-Old-Me Turnpike" become really good at developing excuses, so much so that they begin to deceive themselves. They excuse themselves from any sort of accountability. They barricade themselves against the motivation from others who would like to help them succeed. They refuse to see life through a healthier, more positive lens. Any attempts to encourage them towards taking responsibility for their circumstances are categorically rejected.

Their goal, whether they know it or not, is sympathy. This superhighway leads people to the place where the only comfort they can find in the midst of their horrible circumstances is pity and validation from others. They end up draining their friends and loved ones of all sympathy, however, because their insatiable appetites becomes a never-satisfied desire. Even those who give sympathy can't quite give enough, because these travelers believe that no one has ever had their exact circumstance and that no one could truly understand their pain.

Eventually, they become addicted to the sympathy that they receive and honesty and integrity lose their value. They begin to manufacture versions of stories that will garner them the most pity with less and less attention being paid to the truth of the way things actually unfolded. They lie to themselves, they lie to others, and they live as a constant victim.

Road signs on this superhighway include the constant revisiting of past events and the continuous need for sympathy. Travelers here tend to make many roadside stops to tell others about the hurts of the past.

If you find yourself on this highway, don't beat yourself up. Many of us will get on this highway for a time or even many times throughout our lives. The key is to recognize it and to get off of it.

Exercise: *Have you ever found yourself trapped on the "Poor-Little-Old-Me Turnpike"? Are you on it now? Write down one thing you have pitied yourself for that perhaps you could decide to take responsibility for instead.*

DAY FIFTY-ONE
SUPERHIGHWAYS TO THE LAND OF YOUR NIGHTMARES #6

The final superhighway to the land of your nightmares is one that the vast majority of people travel. It is part of our culture and it is part of our tendency as humans, and it will remain so until we recognize it and strive for something better. I call this superhighway the "You-Don't-Say Expressway".

Travelers on this road *live and talk as though their talk has nothing to do with how they live.*

The "You-Don't-Say Expressway" says that what we talk about really has no effect upon our lives, so we can just talk about whatever we want to talk about. A traveler on this road will reject the idea that speaking things into existence is a reality. She will simply talk about whatever she wants to talk about with whomever she wants to talk about it with and she will have absolutely no concern as to whether or not that talk has any good or bad effects on her life or the lives around her.

She will believe that it is completely acceptable to be sarcastic, to put people down, to be negative, even to tell lies or use fowl language or exaggerate. She will assume that people can tell the difference between when she is joking and when she is being serious and she will use her wit and power with words to appear clever and humorous.

She will also believe that speaking about her worries or fears has no power at all in bringing them about. She will joke about terrible things that may happen and she will attempt to be clever by pointing out negative things about others and about the future.

The most alarming part of this superhighway is that travelers on it cannot see the damage that their words do, even when it is right in front of them. Because they reject the idea that words have power, they do not make the connection in their minds between the things they speak about and the things that are going on around them. They attribute those effects to something else entirely.

Exercise: *We can all find ourselves on the "You-Don't-Say Turnpike" from time to time, speaking about something or someone negatively. Today, write down one person or situation about which you find yourself speaking negatively from time to time and resolve today to speak positive words aloud about that person or situation.*

DAY FIFTY-TWO
COMPARISON REVISITED

Previously, we discussed my belief that comparison is the single most damaging process in human relationships. We are going to revisit comparison today to unpack a few more thoughts on it because this topic is one that can transform a life or a relationship forever.

Comparison is very common in our world. It is a practice used when evaluating employees. What's the measuring stick for evaluating someone? Often it is where you are ranked in certain metrics versus your peers. The same applies for athletes negotiating salary. At the position this athlete plays, how do they compare to others who play the same position? It is clear then that comparison is probably not something we can simply avoid.

So, if we cannot steer clear of it, perhaps we can choose to take a healthy approach to it.

Often when we are trying to improve, we look for people that we admire and try to emulate the things we like about them. We read biographies and try to get to know historic figures or high achieving athletes or business leaders so we have things to aspire to. Or, we connect with a mentor or a leader in our lives and try to learn from them so that we can become like them. This is a good thing, a healthy and productive practice that can push us to become all that we are created to be. However, there is a trap here. If we look at this person we are researching or emulating or following and begin to compare ourselves with them rather than choose to simply incorporate some of their beliefs or practices or strengths into our own lives, we can easily destroy our progress and set ourselves up for failure.

For example, if I begin to get to know a fellow author or business leader whom I admire, it could be a relationship that helps me develop strengths that I still need to hone. However, if I begin to think, *this guy is younger than I am, he's accomplished so much more than I ever have, he's sold more books, he's had a bigger impact*, etc… well, now I've just discouraged myself instead of bettered myself, and very possibly weakened a relationship that could have helped me be a stronger person and even become more of the person I am created to be.

Here's the key: it is never effective to discourage either yourself or someone else based on the comparison of your abilities or beliefs or accomplishments. It is always effective to look upon the abilities or beliefs or accomplishments of others as an inspiration and encouragement for you to be better. And when you have accomplished something great, it is an opportunity for you to use that to encourage rather than discourage the people that will inevitably compare themselves to you.

Exercise: *Is there someone in your life that you compare yourself to and then use that comparison to discourage yourself from becoming a better person? How can you turn that same comparison into something that will encourage you?*

DAY FIFTY-THREE
COMPETITION

Comparison often goes hand in hand with competition. Competition can be a wonderful tool to accomplish things. When we compete against someone, it can be a healthy dynamic where we are both striving for a goal. If we each push ourselves harder to keep up with the other person, the outcome can be that we both win because we both pushed ourselves farther than we would have done had we been doing it alone. However, it can also create a very unhealthy dynamic. When we start to simply want to beat the other person by tearing them down rather than bettering ourselves, we are starting down a path to our own destruction. When the goal of being "better than" becomes a way to avoid criticism, ridicule, or embarrassment, the possibility of healthy synergy is severely limited.

We each have the choice to use competition as something that will help us or hinder us on the path of becoming all that we are created to be.

One way to use competition in a healthy way is as accountability partners. If you each have a goal in the same area, you can encourage each other and push each other farther than if you are doing it alone. With weight loss, for example, this can be a great tool. Decide together on what program you are going to follow, and then check in each day with your accountability partner and give an account of what you ate and your exercise. This is an outstanding way to achieve goals in lots of different areas.

Once again, however, you must be mindful that there is a trap here. Sometimes when I come up short, I look inside to analyze what is wrong with me that I have failed and yet my competitor has succeeded. If I begin to compare with others who have achieved what I am attempting, I could begin to frequently rationalize the advantages they have. For example: *He has more money, so he can purchase healthier food. He has more time, so he can go to the gym whenever he wants. He has more encouragement from his family, so it's easier for him.*

If I don't rationalize it that way, another trap is that I can begin to tear down my competitors. I might undermine their success with cruel comments, harsh judgments, or criticism. Or, I could give them excuses and reasons to slow their progress so that they don't get too far ahead of me. When this dynamic occurs, everybody loses.

There is one other form of competition that can be either healthy or hurtful, depending on how we approach it: self-competition. I really enjoy the sport of golf. One part that makes it so appealing is that I can compete against myself. I've set goals to reach on different courses and I work to achieve them and to score better than I did the last time. I do play with friends but it isn't a competition versus them, I'm just trying to beat my own score. Here, I can strive for my best while also encouraging and helping others to do their best. We can mutually celebrate the victories that we have. The caveat with self-competition is the same as with any other competition: I must compete for the purpose of bettering myself, not discouraging myself.

The conclusion that I have come to is that competition can be a great way to propel myself towards greatness, but only if I focus on the scenarios where everybody wins.

Exercise: *Is there a running mate in your life that you could compete with in a way that would help you both win? What would that competition look like?*

DAY FIFTY-FOUR
VALUES

What do you value in your life?

We don't have the space in a single day's worth of words to discuss a healthy value structure, for that is something that takes a significant amount of self-assessment and deep awareness of our priorities. It is a process that can take months or even years of effort, especially to develop and then hold to a healthy value structure. Today is more of a starting point.

I find it interesting that as I talk with people from time to time about values, many aren't quite sure what that means. There is a tendency to connect the word "value" with *monetary* value almost instantaneously. Value in that sense is what you receive for the money you pay. That is not the sort of value that we want to focus our thoughts on today. The values we approach today are better defined as a person's principles or standards of behavior, or one's judgment of what is most important in life.

It is pivotal to note your initial response to the word "value". What comes to mind? The things that appear first in your thinking may well be the places where you put your highest level of commitment and identity and purpose. Think about what means the most to you in life. These places are probably the areas where you will feel most fulfilled in investing your time and talents.

For me, some of the first things that come to mind in terms of values in life are *relationships and people*. I am mindful of placing the right kind of value on the relationships that I have with my Creator, with family, with friends, with the people I love and the people I respect and the people with whom I invest time. I have discovered that one of the most significant ways to show a person you value them as an individual is to invest *time* with him or her.

There are many other areas of life where humans tend to find value: character, wealth, status, spiritual commitments, achievements, possessions ... and the list just keeps going. If we were to begin compiling a list alphabetically it might look something like this: ability, abundance, acceptance, accessibility, accuracy, achievement, balance, beauty, being the best, belonging, benevolence, boldness, etc.

Today is simply a time to ask yourself the questions: *What do I value? What are the things in my life that are the most important to me? What are the things that draw my attention? What are the things that I most treasure?*

I would encourage you today to invest some time in writing down your values. I have said this before but I will say it again: there is something that happens when we take the time to crystalize our thoughts enough so that they can be written down. These preliminary notes will become important to be aware of and to build our lives on as we continue throughout this study.

When we can come to the point where we can clearly identify an area of our lives in which our highest value is placed, we will be on our way to discovering how we can live life dynamically.

Exercise: *Take the time to write down the things that you value in your life. What is your highest value?*

DAY FIFTY-FIVE
IS IT WORTH IT?

#1: **TIME** ALLOTMENTS

Previously in this book we discussed the question: *Am I willing to pay the price?* It was a question we asked of ourselves when we first began to set some preliminary goals. For the next four days, we will discuss some deeper questions we can ask and answers we can find when we begin to address the worth of any specific goal or vision or purpose. When we first begin to determine if a goal is worth it, we need to figure out what the **time** price tag is. What are the actions that will make our goal a reality? What amount of time will they require? Once we finish this assessment, we can move on to the next step.

A part of the price we will pay when we actively pursue a goal is to realign our allotments of time. If we are going to be more effective and more productive and do more of what we are capable of doing, it means we are going to have to make better use of the time that is available because the reality of it is that there are only 24 hours in a day.

If we are going to go from the place we are to the place we want to be, we have to reallocate our time. Doing this will allow us to get more from each day, each week, and each month as we work towards our goal. If we can be deliberate about scheduling time to work towards our goals, we may discover that the price we are going to pay is not nearly as overwhelming as we originally thought it would be when we first assessed our goals.

So what does this look like, practically speaking?

Depending on how scheduled you are, you probably have at least a rough idea of what your time commitments are for a typical day and week. Things like sleep, work, eating, exercise, driving, investing time with family, watching TV, reading, and other habitual tasks typically take up an average amount of time per day as we go about our lives. This will vary from person to person, and from season to season in life.

When you are ready to commit to the pursuit of a new goal or vision, it is important to decide what parts of your current time allotments you are willing to restructure or sacrifice to make room for the new pursuit. Are you willing to cut out an hour of TV per day to focus on exercise? Are you willing to sacrifice one social night per week out with friends to work on your new business venture?

Whatever it is for you, decide what the new time structure will look like. This will help you determine if it really is worth it and whether or not it holds enough value for you to pay the price.

Exercise: *Think about a goal that feels too overwhelming because of the time it will take. Assess your schedule and determine if you could realign your time allotments so that you can be free to pursue your goal. Is it worth it?*

DAY FIFTY-SIX
IS IT WORTH IT?

#2: **RISK RELATIONSHIP** TESTING

As we prepare to count the costs for what we plan to achieve in life, we must also evaluate our relationships. I refer to this as relationship testing, and there are risks to it. This area is not easy. In fact, from my way of thinking, this may be the most difficult one for many of us.

One of the basic desires of the human being is to be loved. There are certain things that make us feel loved: being accepted by those around us, having them like us, having them approve of us, having the respect us, having them include us in their lives. The value of fulfilling relationships is very important to our balance and happiness in life.

However, when we begin to count the cost, one of the costs involved is that sometimes our realignment of time causes certain relationships to have less time invested. This is not to say that we abandon healthy, life-giving relationships. That would never be an advisable course of action. But sometimes, relationships can look a little different for a season of time. During that season, relationships are tested.

Now a healthy relationship, a true friendship, will not only survive that, but it will thrive on it. A true friend really wants what is best for you. When a friend perceives that you are realigning your time so that you can be more of what you are created to be, so that you can affect the lives of more people, so that you can become a better human being as a result of it, they will rejoice with you. They will support you, encourage you, uplift you, and they will understand that the time sacrifice is worth the end result of you achieving your dream.

I think we are all aware that this is not always the case in every relationship. Some friends can be insecure and will not want to sacrifice time with you. These friends will hold too tightly to you. Some will be jealous, even if they don't say it aloud, and will not want to see you rise to a level of excellence and personhood that they themselves are not willing to rise to. These friends will attempt to pull you down, whether they even realize it or not.

So, there is some testing of relationships that will have to take place in the course of counting the costs. You and I have to make those tough choices. There are people that we spend time with that we should not be spending time with because they do not have our best interest at heart. They are there only when they choose to be there and they are only there to get what they can get, not to contribute to the relationship. Although it is a difficult thing to do, sometimes we have to say good-bye. We have to decide whether or not the dream, goal, purpose, or passion of our life is worth distancing ourselves from relationships that suppress us from becoming all that we are created to be.

Exercise: *Think carefully about your 5 closest friendships. Do these friends support your dream? Is there anyone from whom you need some distance?*

DAY FIFTY-SEVEN
IS IT WORTH IT?

#3: **REARRANGE** YOUR PERSONAL PREFERENCES AND PRIORITIES

After we reallocate our time and assess our relationships, the next thing we need to look at when we decide whether or not something is worth the price is our personal preferences and priorities.

There are just things that we *like* to do, aren't there? There are things that I like to do. There are places I like to go and people I like to be with, and yes, there are just things that I like to do. They are good *for* me, they are good *to* me, and yet I recognize the fact that some of those things that I like to do so much take a disproportionate amount of my time. Now, please understand that I am a great believer in loving my life; life is far too short not to love who you are and what you do. But I am also convinced that there are areas of life that take too much of our time, and we get drawn away into doing things that we enjoy doing simply because we enjoy doing them.

Sometimes these personal preferences start to overtake the things that need to happen in our lives in order to facilitate becoming the people we are created to be. Here's a personal example for you: I know that if I am going to be in a regular habit pattern of physical conditioning, I need to get to that first thing in the morning. If I don't get to it first thing in the morning, it seldom ever happens the rest of the day. Once I head out to my office for the day, I tend to get caught up in the "things" that I do there. These things are good things. Some I enjoy because they are enjoyable, and some I enjoy simply because I am accomplishing things that need to be done. But I can easily lose track of time and end up investing the whole day in the office. I can just get lost in that process of doing the personal preference things at the expense of the other things that I know are good for me.

Perhaps it's a question of priorities. I believe that there is a way to achieve balance in life that allows for both the things we like to do and the things we need to do. That balance begins by rearranging preferences to fit into a priority structure. Would I prefer to relax at my desk in the morning rather than be on treadmill? Yes. However, I can rearrange that preference to a lower priority level than my health.

And here's what I've discovered: when I do make the effort to complete the higher priority items on my agenda, it makes the time that I devote to those things that I enjoy so much more enjoyable. I don't have any lingering guilt, the gnawing in the back of my mind that my enjoyment in one place is costing my betterment in another. I have discovered that I must be willing to step outside of my comfort zone in order to achieve something greater.

Exercise: *Consider your goals. Are there some preferences in your life that have a higher priority level than your goals? Would it be worth it to rearrange those preferences so that you could achieve your goals? Write down some ideas of what that rearrangement could look like for you.*

DAY FIFTY-EIGHT
IS IT WORTH IT?

#4: **RADICALIZE** YOUR HABIT PATTERNS

Once you have determined that there are places in your life where a preference could be moved to a place of lower priority, then you need to begin to look at your habits.

Someone has said, and I think rightly so, that the biggest enemy of a new habit is a current habit. Many experts indicate that most everything we do, we do because of habits. It is unlikely that we will ever just do away with our habits. It is important then that we recognize we have habit patterns and that they are more than just a simple matter of routines we go through in living life.

Oftentimes in this process of living life and striving forward in order to become all that we are created to be, we get slowed down by the habits that are comfortable to us. When we begin to count the cost of achieving our goals, habit patterns play a major role in our evaluation. Sometimes, we recognize our habit patterns are not contributing to our purpose and vision, but we decide that it is easier just to maintain the current habits than it is to force ourselves into something new. Other times, we don't even recognize that we have habit patterns that are stopping us from making the room and priority in life for our dreams and goals.

So what are we to do? Perhaps we must begin by recognizing the fact that by establishing some new habit patterns, we can do away with those that have previously held us back. We can be deliberate about creating new routines that will break the non-productive habits we have formed.

So today, as you move along through the activities of this day, I want you to take a look at the things that you do that are personal preferences. Do those things draw you away from other things that are far more important to do? These are your habit patterns. What are they drawing you to do every day? If they were changed, could it cause you to have a better day and a better year?

If you are willing to actually change your habit pattern in order to accomplish your goal, my assessment is that your goal is indeed worth it.

Exercise: *Consider some of the current habits that you have. Where are these habits really taking you? What 3 habits do you need to get rid of? What 3 new habits do you need to develop?*

DAY FIFTY-NINE
BE YOUR OWN BEST FRIEND

I have learned a truth about life that has helped me in times of great discouragement or loneliness or failure. There is deep importance in choosing to be my own best friend. This is not because others in my life can't encourage me or have deep, intimate, life-giving relationships with me. Rather, it is because if I am not deliberately working to act as my own best friend, I can easily turn into my own worst enemy.

There is a constant interior monologue about ourselves that we listen to. There is one voice that is consistently building us up and encouraging us, and another voice that is consistently belittling us and discouraging us. Those two voices come from the same person, and that person is our own self. And if we are not careful to choose which version of the interior monologue is playing, we can easily fall into the negative version. The fact is that in any situation, in any challenge, in any triumph, there will be both good and bad. There will be things to applaud and admire and celebrate, and there will be things to mock and criticize and scorn.

So, in those moments where we need the positive voice to focus on the good pieces of whatever situation we find ourselves in … are we our own best friend or our own worst enemy? Which voice will we choose to listen to?

I want to learn to be my own best friend. A best friend will encourage me in times of difficulties. A best friend will help me feel better about myself. There are people in my life that make me feel better about myself every single time I am with them. When I leave, I feel more encouraged and empowered about my life and myself and my future. I want to be one of those people – not only for the friends and associates around me, but for myself too.

Today, as you think about you, determine to be your own best friend in good times and in times of challenges. And here's another benefit to making this choice: when you choose to treat yourself this way, you will attract the type of people who want to have those deep, life-giving relationships with you. You will find yourself surrounded with friends who encourage you and lift you up, all because you decided to set that example first by being your own best friend.

Exercise: Consider the interior monologue you have had about yourself today. Are you acting as your own best friend or your own worst enemy? What is one thing you can encourage yourself with today?

DAY SIXTY
WHY DID I DO THAT?

Years ago, before there were seatbelts, I was driving cars. I know it may be hard for some of you younger readers to believe that a) cars ever existed without seatbelts and b) there are still people alive to remember such a world.

But indeed, they did, and I do. When seatbelts came along, they were kind of a novelty, an added feature to a car. Eventually it became evident that seatbelts saved lives and were not a novelty; they were a necessity. So cars began to be manufactured that wouldn't start unless you had the seatbelt fastened. People didn't like that; our independent spirit was challenged. The kill switches were removed and they replaced them with bells and buzzers. Then laws began to be passed and they were there for obviously good reasons.

When my kids and grandkids get into a car, they fasten their seatbelts virtually automatically, every time. But I have to think about it almost every time. It is not an automatic thing for me. In fact, here is the real point of our discussion today: there are times when I find myself knowing I should fasten my seatbelt, thinking about it, driving down the road and yet not fastening the seatbelt! *Why* do I do that? When wisdom, laws, and all the facts agree that that is a better course of action, why do I fight it once in a while?

Why do you fight it? It might not be seatbelts that are your problem. In fact, it probably is not. But perhaps it is making healthy eating choices when you know you struggle with your weight. Or taking your vitamins and supplements on a consistent basis even when you know they make a difference for you. Or tending to a relationship that you know needs a response or an encouragement. Or reading your goals every morning and every evening.

There are things that we know need to be done. We know when to do them. We know why to do them. We know how to do them. Wisdom and facts and experience tell us to do these things, and yet for some reason, we do not do them. So, perhaps today we need to get painfully honest with ourselves and ask the tough questions: *Why do I do that? Is it laziness? Is it pride? Is it a lack of correct priorities? Is it a wrong habit pattern?* As we begin to discover these answers, we are well on our way to changing some things about ourselves and becoming more and more of the people that we are created to be.

Exercise: *Identify a place in your life where you habitually avoid doing something that you know you should do. Why do you do that?*

DAY SIXTY-ONE
PATIENCE

There is an old saying, "Patience is a virtue." I have found this to be a very true statement and one that is valuable to remember on a continual basis. In our world today, we aren't used to waiting. Things move quickly, sometimes almost instantaneously. Our food can be microwaved, our entertainment is on-demand, and our mobile devices can access almost any answer we feel the need to find in mere seconds after we feel the need to find it. Two day shipping is no longer good enough – we've moved to overnight or even same-day. Our society says, *"I want it and I want it now."*

The reality is that although technology has greatly increased the pace at which we live life, there are still certain things that take an investment of time. For example, if I want to learn to play the piano, it's a *process*. I will not take a lesson in the morning and be playing Mozart before lunch. If I have a burning desire to play the piano and I have set it as a goal, I need to be realistic about the type of time investment that will be required to get the result I want. When I set out on the journey, I must realize that I may have setbacks. Perhaps I will struggle with a certain technique and I will need to put in extra hours, days, or weeks to work through my challenges. I must remember—in this scenario and in countless others—I need to have patience both with myself and with the process.

Here is what I observe about others and myself: we frequently give up on our dreams for no other reason than a lack of patience.

Now, playing the piano is a simple illustration, but the need for patience really applies to everything valuable in life. Here are 3 things that I believe to be true:

1. It takes time to change.

2. It takes time to grow.

3. It takes time to develop wisdom.

If there were a pill that we could take that would give us great wisdom, we would probably all take it. If there were a download that we could install in our brain to give us the positive kind of change that we are pursuing, we would probably accept it. If there were an oil or a smoothie or a video or a device or a meme that would make us instantaneously grow into the people we are meant to become, we would all certainly do whatever it took to get it.

Those things do not exist. What we need in order to achieve change and growth and wisdom is *time*.

So, if your dream requires change or growth or wisdom (which all worthwhile dreams are certain to require), then I suggest that you deliberately choose to be patient with yourself and with the process. Celebrate the setbacks and challenges and the time it takes to overcome them. That time invested is taking you ever closer to your dream.

Exercise: *What parts of your becoming are you trying to rush through? How can you slow down and be patient with the process?*

DAY SIXTY-TWO
MOMENTUM

Momentum is often the only difference between winning and losing, between success and failure. It is not talent, or genius or giftedness that allows a person to win or lose on many occasions. Frequently it is simply momentum. When momentum is fueling our attitude and our energy levels, we are inspired to believe that we can rise to a higher level of performance … and so we do. Inherent in the concept of momentum and its power, however, is the understanding that momentum can go in either direction—for us or against us.

Certainly, we desire to create momentum in our lives that brings the essence of our efforts into a powerful force working *for* us rather than *against* us. The desire to have momentum on our side as we journey along the pathway of life requires us to apply a higher standard of accountability and responsibility and passion than that which anyone else might expect or demand.

Momentum in life is not automatic. Positive momentum is something we must constantly strive for, struggle and fight for, if we are to build the kind of a life that will accomplish greatness. In order to build that kind of momentum there will be a continual process of growth and risk. If we are *not* working towards creating positive momentum, we will default to a negative momentum without even realizing it. The most important part of harnessing the power of positive momentum is simply to understand that power. If we realize how important it is, we will be energized to work for it.

Doubt, procrastination, complacency, and a lost sense of purpose in life are the warning signs that appear as momentum turns against us. Faith, action, a passion for excellence, and the single-mindedness of personal purpose guide our pathway to positive momentum that impels us onward. If we establish goals and then give up on them, or if we achieve goals and then feel that we have "arrived" and the challenge is over, we will never have momentum. It is the ongoing process of moving towards a purpose that will create a momentum towards significance in life.

Exercise: *Do you see positive momentum or negative momentum in your life? What areas do you need to be more deliberate about creating positive momentum?*

DAY SIXTY-THREE
SIGNIFICANCE

There is a pathway, a journey to significance and true success in life. This book is a guide to help us find that pathway and to walk down it, whatever it looks like in each of our lives.

You and I live in a society that gives us measuring sticks for success. I talk about it with the young people at Circle A all the time. In the love seminar, we learn about the measuring sticks in our culture being related to money, power, or fame. Are these things the true indicators of success? And why do we even need to have measuring sticks for success?

The experts tell us that we all want to be successful. So, in order to know when we are successful, there's got to be some quantification or qualification to which we can measure ourselves so that we can feel that we are successful.

A number of the quantifiers come in the area of finances. If one has *enough* money, then that individual is successful. Sometimes it is established in the area of power. If one is powerful *enough*, if one controls *enough*, then that person is considered to be successful. Sometimes, the measurement is all about fame. If one is famous *enough*, then he or she is successful. So then the questions become: *How will I know when I am successful? How will I know when it's enough?*

I happen to believe that none of those three criteria is a good measuring stick for significance and real success in life. Yes, they may be indicators of what our society and culture believe to be "success". But is that sort of success what really matters in life? For me, it is not. Money, power, and fame have never brought me a deep sense of significance or purpose in life.

And so, in my journey to significance—and I repeat once again, this is my personal perspective—there is no real success in life without significance. Significance has nothing to do with how much money I can accumulate. It has nothing to do with how many people I control or have power over. It has nothing to do with how many people know me or don't know me.

Now, I will confess to you that I enjoy having the experience every once in a while of seeing my impact on the world. For example, I was driving across the Skyway Bridge in Tampa one day, listening to myself on a CD. I don't do that often, but that day I had myself playing. As I pulled up to pay the toll, I lowered the window on my car and the lady at the tollbooth said, "Excuse me is that Skip Ross you are listening to?"

I said, "It is."

She said, "He's really good, isn't he?"

I said, "He is! Have a great day!" I closed my window and drove off. I never told her that I am Skip Ross! That kind of experience happens more often to me now in various parts of the world. One time recently, I met some people from the Arctic Circle in an airport in Sweden who had been listening to some audios I've recorded. Does

that make me famous and successful? No. What it does mean is that I have a chance to be significant, at least in the lives of some people. *You have that same opportunity.* Whoever you are, you have that same kind of chance. You may not influence people from the Arctic Circle, but you may influence somebody in your family or church or school or job. You may change his or her life for the better.

I can think of no better way to experience and achieve significance in life than to know that my life positively impacts another life, or two, or hundred, or thousand, for the better.

Exercise: *What do you envision as the definition of significance for you?*

DAY SIXTY-FOUR
ROADBLOCKS TO SIGNIFICANCE

INTRODUCTION

It was in one of the smaller meeting rooms at a Holiday Inn near Pittsburgh, Pennsylvania and I remember the evening as though it were yesterday. It actually was a number of years ago and I was conducting one of my early *Dynamic Living* seminars. In those days, the seminar would take the entire weekend. They were marathon sessions!

I am always interested to know why people choose to come and invest time with me to study these principles and on this particular evening I decided to ask the question. So, I asked the people in attendance, "Why did you come? What is it that you wish to accomplish as a result of having been here this weekend and what difference do you want it to make in your life as you continue this adventure of personal development?"

As you might well imagine, I got a variety of responses that evening. One of the young men made a statement that is as fresh and relevant today as it was then, even though it was many years ago. Here was his statement: "Skip, all of my life I have felt I had potential and ability. I have observed, however, that I continually seem to fall short of the goals and the aspirations I have for my life. The reason I came tonight is to see if you can help me discover what it is that causes me to continually hold myself back rather than to propel myself forward into my dreams."

I can't say I have thought about that statement every day of my life since then, but I can say I have thought about it *frequently*. What is it that causes me to hold myself back from achieving my goals and dreams? What holds me back from significance?

Can I be honest? It is certainly my opinion that without honesty about this subject or any other, we won't proceed very far. So here's my straightforward approach: at this writing, I'm not convinced that I'm ready to share what I believe to be some of the answers for this question of why we hold ourselves back. I'm not convinced that I am the master of what I think I need to master in order to do some teaching on this particular topic. It is, however, so important that the lack of perfection in my experience should not deter us from the discussion.

So, let's commit the next several days to exploring the question, *What holds us back from significance?* There is a pathway of potential to our purpose and significance in life. If we are uncertain as to where we want to go in life, the obstacles are insurmountable. But even when we have a clear direction, there are still major roadblocks that get in the way of our significance. I have identified twelve, and I am delighted to share them with you.

Exercise: *Before you embark on the study of roadblocks for the following days, think about why and how you might be holding yourself back. Are there answers that clearly come to you?*

DAY SIXTY-FIVE
ROADBLOCKS TO SIGNIFICANCE

#1: LACK OF **PERSONAL INTEGRITY**

The roadblock on the highway to significance in life that is most powerful, in both my observation of myself and other people, is the lack of personal integrity. As we learned before, integrity means being consistent, or congruent, on the inside and the outside of one's life.

Now you begin to see why I draw such a contrast between significance and success. As you and I look around the world in which we live, we see people who are successful— at least, as most people measure success. There are millionaires, there are billionaires, and there are people who possess vast amounts of power or fame who are not people of integrity at all. And so to say that you have to be a person of integrity in order to be considered to be successful as most people count success … well, we all know that that's just not true. But to be a person of *significance*, in my opinion, one has to continually fight this battle with one of the biggest roadblocks there is in life's journey to significance: integrity.

Here's the bottom line: when word, thought and deed are consistently congruent, we have integrity. *Word, thought, and deed.*

The thought life may be the least obvious to others and yet it is perhaps the most influential upon the individual himself. For example, if a person says he believes in the power of goal-setting, he teaches the strategies of goal setting, he projects to the world that he practices goal-setting, and yet never actually engages the process for himself in his own life – that is a stark lack of integrity. Not only will it eventually destroy his platform and influence, but it will build self-doubt into him. But even one step further: *if he even does the deed* of practicing goal setting but doesn't truly *believe* in it, doesn't actually think it works like he teaches that it works … that is still a lack of integrity, and it is still highly destructive.

One might well ask then, "Are there ways by which I can improve my thought process and thereby protect and strengthen my integrity?" I believe there are many. Invest your life in truth, and then bring your words in conformity with that standard. Develop generous portions of patience, forgiveness, and humility. Focus your life on moral and ethical actions. Build relationships with friends and mentors who hold the same approach to life. Cultivate a boldness for doing the right thing, and do it even when the cost is high. Remember that this pursuit of integrity is not about perfection; it is about persistence, excellence, and commitment.

If we choose to live with a lack of integrity, we will find ourselves staring at a giant impasse of a roadblock on the path to significance. But when we become people of integrity, our significance in life will be substantial.

Exercise: *Is there an area of your life where a lack of personal integrity has become a roadblock for you? What steps can you take to overcome it?*

DAY SIXTY-SIX |
ROADBLOCKS TO SIGNIFICANCE |

#2: COMPETITIVE **COMPARISON**

This roadblock stands in direct opposition to the principle that we teach in the *Dynamic Living* seminar called the principle of giving. This principle is summarized by the thought, "Give and you will receive." When we grasp the beauty and the importance of giving, we will reap huge rewards in life. The roadblock comes when we begin to *keep score*. The giving of my time, compliments, encouragement, help or resources is hugely beneficial unless it is carefully calculated on the basis of how it will impact *me*. Competitive comparison produces at least four results in our lives that are highly destructive to the process of achieving significance.

First of all it **creates condemnation**. When I begin to compare myself with other people, I could begin to feel arrogant, thinking that I am better than they are because of all I have given. On the other side of the coin, I could also begin to feel worthless. I could assume that because my giving was not reciprocated, I must not be worth giving to. Either way, I am condemning either them or myself.

The second thing it does is to **corrupt character**. When we begin condemning others or ourselves, it begins to corrupt our character. The roadblock is set up and we are no longer free or open people. We begin to play the "blame game". We begin to try and hide the flaws that exist within our experience of life. This causes us to compromise our integrity, and thus our character is corrupted.

The third thing competitive comparison does is to **corrode courage**. If we think we are better than other people, then when we face those tough situations of life that require deep and abiding relationships, we find it difficult to trust people that we deem somehow beneath us. And if our courage fades away with people that we have felt superior to, it obviously will disappear with people we think are better than we are. Let me clarify. Here is what I have discovered about people in school, in business, in marriages, in life: I observe that there are a lot of people who simply do not move on towards something better in those various areas of their lives because they are afraid to really give it their best effort. Their courage is corrupted because of the competitive comparison they have bought in to for so long.

Finally, competitive comparison **confuses our convictions**. If we feel we are better than other people, if we feel we are not as good as other people, if we feel like we have compromised our integrity or lost our courage, then our convictions are confused. Our commitment to our life, our business, our family, our future, our dreams, and our hopes is *confused*. We lose sight of who we are and where we are going and the focus of our purpose is muddled.

I have watched life fall apart for people who simply get distracted by the compulsion to compare themselves with others. This comparison somehow gives them the justification to drop out of their vocation, out of a marriage, out of school, or out of any other part of their life where they feel threatened. And we don't see them anymore. Why? They gave up. They are roadblocked from significance.

Exercise: *Are there people in your life that you tend to compare yourself with? Has that become a roadblock for you? What steps can you take to overcome it?*

DAY SIXTY-SEVEN
ROADBLOCKS TO SIGNIFICANCE

#3: **LOOSE** TALK

Loose talk is the most frequently constructed roadblock in the lives of people. It develops around the reluctance to believe that what we say makes a difference. There are many people who have a distinct unwillingness to even *notice* what it is that is coming out of our mouths, let alone agree to the proposition that it truly matters. Despite aversion to or acceptance of this truth, the truth remains: our words have a direct and profound effect on our lives.

So what experience of life do we speak of? Are we talking about the things we *want* to happen? Or are we talking about the negative things that we *don't want* to happen? When we start talking about our business, our relationships, our future, our health, our hopes and dreams, there is a question that must constantly be asked. This is how I put it to myself, "Skip, is that what you want?"

Are we verbalizing what we really want? Are we talking about growth? Are we talking about solutions? Are we talking about success and significance? Or are we just letting our mouths run unfiltered with negative thoughts and emotions and "venting"? Loose talk!

The fact of the matter is that this particular area of our lives is even more complicated and difficult than what I have thus far indicated. There is an even more important question, the question that underlies every word that comes out of our mouths: "What is the *thought* process that is creating the flow of words that I am speaking?" The scriptures tell us that whatever is going on inside of our hearts will be revealed by what we talk about.[9] So the roadblock to significance in our lives that is associated with loose talk really begins in our minds. Therefore the designation for this roadblock might better be titled — loose thought, loose talk!

We sometimes act as though it doesn't make any difference what we say or what we think, when actually it makes all the difference in the world. Not only does it affect our environment, our attitude, the sorts of people we attract, our energy level, our credibility, and our productivity, it also directly affects the actual events that occur in our lives. I have observed countless incidents in my life and the lives of others where an event has been spoken into existence. I have taught for years that whatever you talk about will happen … so watch out what you say!

What are we creating and affirming by the way we think and the way we speak? Is it laser-focused thought and talk about the things we really want? Is it directed towards the ingredients that will give us significance and purpose in life? Or is it loose thought and loose talk about anything and everything that pops into our minds and meddles with our emotions?

It makes a difference.

Exercise: *Is there an area of your life where loose talk or loose thought has become a roadblock for you? What steps can you take to overcome it?*

DAY SIXTY-EIGHT
ROADBLOCKS TO SIGNIFICANCE

#4: **NEGATIVE** BELIEF

For a long time in my life, I thought in terms of belief versus doubt. The teaching I had, the reading I did, and the observation of people living around me seemed to make that a well-reasoned conclusion. I always wanted to come down on the side of belief and not on the side of doubt.

And then one day, I had one of those kind of experiences in life that we sometimes call the "aha" moment and it caused my thinking to change. When our thinking changes, everything changes. I saw this whole area of life from a different perspective. Instead of thinking about previously simple distinctions between faith and doubt, it became far more powerful to think in terms of experiencing either *negative belief* or *positive belief*. I realized that we all believe something about our lives and our future and ourselves. It is not a *lack* of belief that we must fight against; it is the choice to allow our belief to turn *negative* that will become the roadblock.

We construct our lives based on the beliefs that we hold. If we can understand that our lives are being built on either a faith in the negative or faith in the positive, we will harness a deeper awareness of the true power of belief. When I began to appreciate the fact that I was expressing faith in the positive or faith in the negative, it made a huge difference for me. I began to look for and listen for ways to express positive belief, knowing that if I chose to express what I had previously viewed as doubt, it was actually still expressing a belief … a belief in my own failure.

There is great wisdom in the counsel that encourages us to catch ourselves in the process of building a foundation of faith and then to determine whether it is faith in a negative outcome or faith a positive outcome. When we are working to develop confidence in what *can't* happen, or in the things we *don't* want to happen, we are roadblocked. When we begin to understand this concept, we are empowered to know the source of many of our roadblocks. And with this new insight we are equipped to be able to stop building roadblocks and then to demolish those that we have already built.

Remember, the good thing about life is that we always have a choice. We have a choice in the investment of our belief. We can choose to believe in what is true and honorable, right and pure, lovely and admirable. We can invest our faith in things that are excellent and worthy of praise and consistent with our hopes and dreams and visions for our future. The roadblocks come when we begin to accumulate belief in those things that are false, things that are filled with impossibility, things that place our focus upon our weaknesses and failures, things that find the worst to assume and believe instead of the best. When we recognize that this is a proactive and habit-forming style of belief, we can stop placing our belief on the negative side of the ledger anytime we choose. And for me, that is NOW.

Exercise: *Is there an area of your life where negative belief has become a roadblock for you? What steps can you take to overcome it?*

DAY SIXTY-NINE
ROADBLOCKS TO SIGNIFICANCE

#5: **NONPRODUCTIVE** RELATIONSHIPS

We become like the people with whom we associate. Period. End of story. But you say, "Wait a minute, Skip. That can't be the end of the story." Yes, it is. The end of the story. We can't escape it. We can't change it. We can only recognize the power of the choices we make about the relationships that we build, and then be guided by that knowledge as we choose the people with whom we will invest our time and hearts and dreams. The people in our closest circles of relationship are the ones who will set the environment in which we will live.

Our relationships can make us or break us. This is a rather easy principle to observe in the people around us. We perceive that an individual who generally is very open and honest can change at an alarming rate when placed in an environment of friends that feel differently about integrity. We see people who once expressed heartfelt encouragement become people who find humor in cruel putdowns. These opposing worldviews and values can come from the same individual who has simply changed spheres of influence.

If you have ever felt the pressure of friends who unknowingly influence you to be a lesser version of yourself, then you understand the power of this roadblock. People often tend to try to ignore or belittle the power and the strength of this obstacle to significance in life. We are better to realize that its power comes from precisely that: a belief that says *it doesn't make any difference*. We can overcome the power of this roadblock by choosing to remember that it truly does make a difference. We can then carefully select the people with whom we associate, and we can nurture those relationships that move us along toward significance.

The challenge with nonproductive relationships does not merely arise when we are dealing with people. There are nonproductive relationships with things and activities as well. These might include what we watch, what we listen to, and what we read. As certainly as people can have a relationship with another human being, people can have a relationship with a video game or a television show. Now, I'm not opposed to video games or television, but if the relationship with a video game begins to overshadow a relationship with people or with your future or with your dreams, it is a non-productive relationship and it is a major roadblock on the journey to significance in life.

We are wise if we begin to understand relationships in life mean something—in fact, they can mean almost everything. They affect us profoundly and we rise to the heights or fall to the depths of the relationships that we build.

Exercise: *Do you have non-productive relationships in your life that have become roadblocks for you? What steps can you take to disengage from them?*

DAY SEVENTY
ROADBLOCKS TO SIGNIFICANCE

#6: TAKING YOUR EYES OFF THE **ROAD**

When I was about 26 years old, I was living in Los Angeles, California. I was driving the L.A. freeways, and if you've ever driven the L.A. freeways in a fast rush hour—which means bumper to bumper at 55-65 miles an hour—you know what a thrilling experience it is! In fact I got so good at it, I had at one point thought I could probably become a racecar driver. I would drive on the Los Angeles expressways with my steering wheel held by my knees, balancing a book on the steering wheel with the music that I was memorizing for the next concert I would be giving.

I don't do that anymore, of course. First of all, it's become an illegal act and secondly, I find that if I take my eyes off the road now, I tend to get off track. In fact there are cars now that will sound alarms at you if you begin to shift lanes on the highway without a turn signal on (I happen to drive one). Car manufacturers have recognized that if one takes one's eyes off the road, an accident is likely.

Unfortunately, we have not yet invented or developed an off-track warning alarm system for our personal lives. We don't have a built-in sensor that will let us know when we have taken our eyes off our goals.

There are many reasons that people can become trapped by this roadblock. Some have just never understood the goal-setting process very well, so they don't have a clear vision of their goal. Sometimes people might have been told about effective ways to set goals, but they don't actually implement them, and again they lack a clear vision. Sometimes they have gone through the process of setting goals effectively, but they have become distracted by something else. In any of these cases, the common theme is that their eyes are not on the road they must travel to achieve their goal.

When we take our eyes off the road and refuse to be steadfastly unwavering in our commitment to goal-setting and the visualization of our dreams, when we refuse to dream or deny the existence of our dream, when we don't know where we are going, when we don't feel like we have a purpose in life, then we have hit the roadblock.

So the question becomes: what is the dream that will inspire you to keep your eyes on the road? What element of your significance in life is stronger than your doubts and distractions and fears? Find it, see it, and hold onto it. Keep your eyes on the road.

Exercise: *Is there a goal or dream that you were heading for and then you took your eyes off the road? Is it worth finding the road again?*

DAY SEVENTY-ONE
ROADBLOCKS TO SIGNIFICANCE

#7: ELIMINATING THE **PHOTO SPOTS**

I remember our family's first trip to Yosemite National Park when I was just a youngster. We came through the tunnel that opens up to a magnificent view of the mountain-ringed valley. There was an area specially constructed at the side of the road marked with signs that said *Scenic View—Photo Spot*. Indeed! It was breathtaking - there was Half Dome in all of its splendor. It is still a setting of profound visionary influence in my life and I will always remember stopping at the photo spot to take in the view. Places of inspiration around the world are marked with those signs. Often, the most beautiful and memorable views of a particular location can be found at these markers.

The inspiration we derive from the memories wrapped up in the photo spots of life is invaluable as we move towards significance. Life has its ups. Life has its downs. Life has its great moments and life has its challenges. Life is like that. You're going to experience this. I'm going to experience this. Because we are alive and human, we will experience the moments of great happiness and exhilaration, and we will also experience the dark times of obstruction and difficulty.

So when the challenges of life come, where do we go? Where is our place of inspiration? Sometimes it's a place with a physical location. Sometimes it's a place in our mind. And yet, there are a lot of people who have never figured out a place where they can go. I decided a long time ago that I need places to go, places that I can get to at a moment's notice. Sometimes it's by thought. Sometimes it's by picture. Sometimes it's by music. Sometimes it's by people. And sometimes it's being physically present in a location.

There is a place that Susan and I visit every year in Honolulu, Hawaii. It's one of our favorite places on earth. Although we do physically travel there each year, I can also go to the *House Without a Key* in Waikiki just by thinking about it. There are also times when I go to the Los Angeles freeways. You may think that is strange. You may even ask, *why?* I will tell you. It is because in the days when I was engaged with the most intense fights with fear in my life, I would drive hour after hour on those freeways singing, praying, and repeating affirmations which would bring inspiration back into my life. I can still travel there in my mind to celebrate the victories I enjoyed in those days, and the memories of those victories become inspiration for my present circumstances.

I don't know where you will go for inspiration. Maybe it's a book. Maybe it's an audio in some format. Maybe it's a memory of a victory won. What I know is this: if you don't have a place of inspiration to go to, you have a serious roadblock. Life has lots of "stuff" to throw in your pathway. Significance is found in the midst of the "stuff" of life. So take the time to crystallize the inspirational photo spots along the way, and don't forget to revisit them frequently.

Exercise: *What are the photo spots that you have encountered along the journey of your life? How can you be deliberate about returning to them?*

DAY SEVENTY-TWO
ROADBLOCKS TO SIGNIFICANCE

#8: **ACCELERATING** IN NEUTRAL

When I began to write about this roadblock, I debated between a lot of "L" words. Listless. Lazy. Lug. Lout. Lethargic. Lifeless. Languorous. At one point I thought I would just use all of them. It would've sounded something like this: if I am a listless, lethargic, lazy, lifeless, languorous lout then I am facing a massive roadblock! Well, I determined that I couldn't possibly call myself that nor could I accuse anyone else of it!

So here's a better, more positive expression of the same problem: there are many of us whose journey to success and significance in life can be roadblocked when we try to drive in neutral. Regardless of how much we seek to convince ourselves and others that we are working to move forward in life, we will remain where we are if there is no accountability and responsibility for *action*. We may feel or at least pretend that we are "putting the pedal to the metal", but talk and hype do not equate to action.

One of the major road signs we look for that warns us that this roadblock is coming up is the use of *excuses*. Whenever we find ourselves in the process of trying to "explain away" what's going on in our lives, we are approaching the roadblock. Whenever we find ourselves looking for other people and circumstances to blame for our lack of progress, we are approaching the roadblock. When we rationalize and seek to justify our lack of a consistent hard work ethic, we are approaching the roadblock. The unfortunate thing is that it is possible to look very "busy" and still be totally roadblocked. It is possible to convince many people around us—and even ourselves— that we are on the right track. There is no progress on this track, however, because we have become unaccountable, unteachable, and irresponsible. We can be so distracted by the urgent things in our lives that we miss what is really important. Urgent things almost always require massive amounts of our energy, but often they are not crucial to the priorities we have identified.

When the tires are spinning and the engine is roaring but we are not moving towards significance, we need to take a step back and evaluate where we are investing our time and how we are taking our action.

Exercise: *Is there an area of your life where accelerating in neutral has become a roadblock for you? What steps can you take to overcome it?*

DAY SEVENTY-THREE
ROADBLOCKS TO SIGNIFICANCE

●

#9: LOOKING FOR THE **SHORTCUTS**

In my preparation for this segment, I thought about many of my own experiences. And then, just last night, I had a dream that illustrated what I was trying to write about. Funny how that happens. I was driving in Hawaii and I was in a hurry. I'm not sure if it was to catch a flight or to see a sunset, but I know I was in a hurry. Someone in the car, and it could've been a voice coming from the dashboard, told me to follow a certain road. I thought to myself, *I know a shortcut*, and I proceeded to follow it. Now, you probably know what happened next. It took a while, but eventually I realized this would not take me to the airport or the sunset. As the road narrowed and the terrain got rougher, I was suddenly face-to-face with a chain link fence roadblock.

I am confident that you have had a similar experience. You know that feeling that develops in the pit of your stomach. It is a disheartening realization when you discover that you have tried to bargain with the pathway to your goal. You took a shortcut, and by doing so only made the goal more difficult to achieve. J.R.R. Tolkien in the *Fellowship of the Ring* wrote, "Short cuts make long delays".[10]

The illustration of the shortcut while driving a car is one that we are all familiar with, but oftentimes it does not have serious consequences. However, when we are talking about the pathway to significance in life, the seeking of shortcuts to get there becomes a major roadblock in completing the vision. Life demands determination and hard work. There is no shortage of evidence that many people do, in fact, try shortcuts. Unfortunately we only have a momentary glimpse of their experience with the shortcut as they speed by on their own pathway to their purpose in life. If we could see the whole process from start to finish, we would undoubtedly see that the shortcuts would never led us to the finish.

Is it a legitimate thing to ask the question, *Is there a better way?* I believe the answer to that is a resounding yes. Our creativity and imagination certainly make it possible for us to continue to find better ways. The distinction between finding a better way and seeking a way to avoid the things that are required is a differentiation that is crucial if we are to find significance in life. We should always work to find the best, most effective, most efficient, most empowering way to our dreams – and then we should give it everything we've got. When we give our full enthusiasm to the process we have embraced, significance is well within reach.

Exercise: *Is there an area of your life where looking for shortcuts has become a roadblock for you? What steps can you take to overcome it?*

DAY SEVENTY-FOUR
ROADBLOCKS TO SIGNIFICANCE

#10: LACK OF **SELF-DISCIPLINE**

In the *Dynamic Living* seminar, we talk about the principle of self-discipline. *"Do what needs to be done, when it ought to be done, whether you like it or not."* The fact of the matter is that we will all be disciplined in life. Discipline has never been optional. Discipline will either be supplied from an outside source or from within ourselves. We are not talking so much in terms of *punishment* as we are in terms of restraint and willpower. When a child is small, the divinely appointed messenger of discipline is the parent. The goal of that process it is to build within the child a value structure that will enable him to become self-disciplined as he develops. During those maturing years as the internalization process continues, there are various people and institutions that stand in the position of administering whatever discipline may be needed. The more rebellious he becomes towards that process, the less likely it is that he will internalize his own discipline. If he does not internalize it, if he does not learn to become self-disciplined, he will hit a roadblock on the journey to significance.

Self-discipline is all about becoming the master of doing the things we prefer not to do. It is not difficult to remember to do the things that we enjoy. It is not difficult to do the things that we perceive are of value to us. The whole concept of internalized discipline carries with it the understanding that this is not a one-time thing. Self-discipline requires sustained, perpetual, massive action. If that sounds like an every day, every moment kind of thing, that's because I believe that's what it is. There are some who pretend to find a false sense of comfort in saying that some are just given a more disciplined spirit than others. But discipline is not something we are born with; rather it is something we develop. Our every day actions can initiate, reinforce, enhance, and refine that state of inner self-discipline.

Here's what a self-disciplined mind says: "It's time for me to do this, it's time for me to go there, it's time for me to do that, it's time for me to make the right choice in regard to this next step, it's time for me to follow my priorities in life. These are the right things to do, and so I will do them whether I like it or not."

If we don't internalize the discipline and do it because it is the best thing for us to do, then clearly there are difficulties ahead. No one else can discipline us into significance. If we are going to achieve the becoming of the best versions of ourselves, then we are going to need to put in the effort, dedication, and purposeful commitment to the process that it will take to get there.

Exercise: *Are you a self-disciplined person? In what areas could you be better?*

DAY SEVENTY-FIVE
ROADBLOCKS TO SIGNIFICANCE

#11: THE **NEW DRIVER** SYNDROME

When I was 11 years old, I learned to drive by driving a pickup truck on my grandfather's wheat farm. It was 640 acres of nothing but wheat, so I couldn't do too much damage. My grandfather told me to go ahead with it, and he didn't have to ask me twice! As I attempted to drive out across that field, it was not pretty. The driving, I mean. The landscape was beautiful. At least … it was before I began to mow it down. I don't know if you've ever watched someone who is just learning to drive a stick-shift vehicle, but it can be quite a spectacle.

A new driver is very uncertain as to how hard to push the gas, how quickly to disengage the clutch, and when to go for the brake in order to remain in control of the vehicle. So, it becomes a process of pushing too hard and backing off, and pushing too hard and backing off, and pushing too hard and backing off. And lurching thusly through the fields, I slowly started learning to drive.

I found that the coordination between the clutch and the gas and my brain and my foot was not an easy thing to learn. I sometimes wonder if the challenge I have had with my neck, which I have experienced a good portion of my life, might have had its origin in those wild and uncontrolled days of that 11 year old boy. After the first drive to the barn across that field, I might well have given up and concluded I could not accomplish this thing. I could have become so embarrassed and discouraged by the laughter from my uncle and my grandfather that I might have refused to try again.

Here was the process: push and let off, push and let off, push and let off. People do that in life as well, and it is a major roadblock to significance. Sometimes when people are a not good at a task when they first begin, their initial inability causes them to back off and give up. *Roadblock!* Sometimes people just deny the importance of the principle of action. They work really hard for a season and then they procrastinate. They make an initial effort and then they get distracted. *Roadblock!* It happens all the time. We approach a task with enthusiasm and then someone laughs. We lay out our plans with hope and belief and then someone tells us that it can't be done. Push and back off. Push and back off.

Here's what I've learned works best for me: "I will—UNTIL!"

Exercise: *Do you see evidence of new driver syndrome in your life? What steps can you take to persist through the temptation to stop and start?*

ROADBLOCKS TO SIGNIFICANCE

#12: LEAVING YOUR HAND ON THE **SCALE**

In life, it's just better to do what's right.

There is a principle of fairness that has existed since the creation of mankind. I know what's right. You know what's right. I know how to treat people. You know how to treat people. Why? Because we are people. And here's what I've learned: any time I try to *keep from doing* what I know to be the right thing to do, or when I *make excuses* about not doing the right thing, or I pretend that I *don't know* what the right thing to do is, I am placing my hand on a scale to favor it in my direction.

And that's not fair.

Life was not meant to be lived like that, and behaving in that manner is a major roadblock to significance in life. Are there people who cheat and still accumulate wealth? Yes. Are there people who lie and still accumulate power? Yes. Are there people who steal or disparage others or manipulate and still accumulate fame and notoriety? Yes. But how about significance? I would venture to guess that the people who have had the greatest positive influence in your life are those who have learned the principle of fairness and who practice it regularly. It is not fair to seek significance in life by doing something that is weighing the scales in your favor at the expense of somebody else. A significance bought with such actions would be no significance at all.

So we have learned about twelve roadblocks to significance. I'll close with this thought. As I have been writing these—reading, studying, evaluating myself—there are times when I get in the midst of it all and I realize how much yet there is to learn, apply, and get good at. I am grateful for the progress made. I am grateful for the opportunity to continue to move along this journey to significance, but if I am not careful, I'll get tough on myself. What I have discovered about that is that when I get tough on myself it begins to rob me in other areas of my life. I become less effective here and less effective there. I become more stressed here and more stressed there. Does it impact my marriage? Absolutely. Does it impact me physically? Absolutely. So, I must remember that I am a work in progress, and that significance will come one tiny step at a time.

I would not want any of you to leave these pages thinking, "Wow! I've got 12 roadblocks on my pathway. I don't know if I can ever make it." No. I want you to leave these pages today thinking this: "There are roadblocks on my journey to significance in life and now I am a little bit more aware, and therefore, I can travel that much better on my journey."

Exercise: Which of the 12 roadblocks stands out to you as the one that you need the most focus on? What is one change you can make today?

DAY SEVENTY-SEVEN
REFUSE INFERIORITY

Eleanor Roosevelt said, "Remember, no one can make you feel inferior without your consent".[11] Wow, what a powerful statement! Nobody has the power to make you feel inferior unless you tell them it's okay to do so.

Feelings of inferiority are certainly crippling if we allow them into our lives. If we perceive that we are not "as good as" the people with whom we associate, we will never work very hard at becoming the best version of ourselves in that environment. So let's ask some questions about this thought then. First of all, why do people try to make other people feel inferior? And secondly … why would I give anyone permission to do that to me?

There is no doubt that we will all run into people in our lives that will try to make us feel inferior. Unfortunately, it is a coping technique that some people have adopted; some do it deliberately and directly, others do it without thinking much about how their words and attitudes belittle the people around them. If someone feels inferior themselves, they frequently believe that they will feel better about themselves when they have intimidated the other person to feel lesser. If they can knock someone else down to a place of inferiority, somehow they believe that they will feel more valuable. It rarely works out this way—in fact, I believe that it never works out this way. There are, however, many in our society who find themselves caught in the vicious cycle of tearing others down in order to claw their own way to the top.

Here's the truth we need to remember: there is no one in the world that can make you feel inferior unless you give your permission for them to do so.

So why would you give them the permission? The only reason you would or *could* give anyone else that consent is if you have already given it to yourself. If you give yourself permission to feel inferior, you have opened the floodgates for anybody at any time to contribute to those feelings of inferiority. If you speak to yourself as someone who is less valuable than others, then anyone who adds to that conversation is only building off a base that you have constructed.

And so today, refuse. Refuse to give that permission to anyone, *including yourself.* You are a beautiful and wonderfully unique creation of God himself. You are not inferior. So live today in that truth!

Exercise: *Think of a person who tries to make you feel inferior. What steps do you need to take to disallow that input into your life?*

DAY SEVENTY-EIGHT
CONFLICT

It is no secret to those who know me that I am a peacemaker. I pursue peace. I would far rather not have to ever experience conflict and I go to great lengths to control the atmosphere in which I live so that it is as peaceful and as without conflict as possible. We all know people who feel very differently about life. Oftentimes, simply by looking at someone's countenance or listening to the tone of his or her voice, we can identify that he or she is headed for a conflict. These approaches to conflict are two distinctly different "camera views" of life: one can lead to a victim mentality and an irresponsible lack of engagement; the other can lead to anger, arrogance, and destruction. Neither extreme gives us a very healthy approach to life. Fortunately, there is a third camera angle. Max Lucado points out in his book, *When God Whispers Your Name*, "Conflict is inevitable, but combat is optional."[12]

If we ignore the existence of conflict in the territory surrounding our journey to significance, we assure ourselves the inability to arrive at our destination. So whether we flee at the first sign of confrontation or explode at the slightest provocation, we lock ourselves into a pattern of *reaction* that will never take us where we want to go. The habitual mindset that says "this cannot be resolved" is self-destructive and is also catastrophic to our relationship building. If life revolves around relationships, then conflict resolution becomes one of the vital skills of life.

The resolution of differing ideas, opinions, values and actions that have the potential of erupting into warfare begins first of all within each one of us. When I approach a conflict, I am best positioned for the resolution of that conflict if I have an attitude that humbly accepts my shortcomings, resolutely demands a period of non-defensive listening for understanding, joyfully anticipates the added value that the eventual resolution will bring to my life, and confidently embraces the expectation that there is opportunity in every difficulty.

When our determination is to add value to everyone we meet and to believe that everyone we meet has something of value to contribute to our lives, we see life differently than most people see it. When revenge, aggression and retaliation are the goal, reconciliation is nearly impossible. The more incompetent one feels or the more egotistically arrogant one pretends to be, the more likely it is there will be an unresolved conflict.

So then, we are not so much disturbed by things, situations, or circumstances as we are by the camera angle through which we see them. When we're willing to look through the camera and see ourselves first, we are better equipped to see and understand others. We are than empowered to *respond* rather than *react* and to learn from the experience.

The possibilities of successful conflict resolution are beautifully expressed in the words of Henry David Thoreau: "Could a greater miracle take place than for us to look through each other's eyes for an instant?"[13] That takes forethought. That takes courage. That takes a humble mindset. And sometimes, that takes a reassessment of everything that's involved in the conflict.

Exercise: *Are you engaged in a conflict or potentially headed into a conflict that could use a reassessment and a new perspective? What would that look like?*

DAY SEVENTY-NINE
PRIORITIES #1

Today we will take a closer look at the priorities in our lives. This is a topic that could take a whole book—or even multiple books—but our space is small and our time is short. We will take the next several days to think about it, and then I will encourage you to do some more reading and thinking on your own about this very important part of life.

Priorities already exist in our lives, whether we acknowledge them or not. The real question is, have we been deliberate about establishing them or have we simply allowed the circumstances and relationships that surround us to create an ever-changing pattern of priorities? Have we determined what is decisively pivotal to us or have we let the ebb and flow of life determine that for us?

Knowing what my priorities are helps me organize my schedule and makes for much easier decision-making. Now you may be thinking, *Skip, I know things that are important to me, but I don't know which one is more important than the other?* That's okay. Many don't. Determining your priorities in life is a process that takes focused effort.

We often have sessions about priorities during our staff training time in the summers. During one of these sessions, a Leadership Team member shared something from the film *A Few Good Men*. During the movie, one of the Marines explains the Marine code: Unit, Corps, God, Country.[14] What this means is that he gives his loyalty—up to and including his life itself—in that order. I am not in the Marines, so this is not my personal code, but it is an example of a group of people who have a clear delineation of and commitment to a hierarchy of priorities.

I have come up with an acrostic for the word "Priorities" that will help us delve a little deeper into our understanding of this topic. Let's begin.

P = Personalize Preferences. What do you genuinely enjoy doing? There are things in life that, if given the choice, we would prefer to do. For example, if I have a choice between playing a round of golf or doing my workout, my preference would be to play golf. So what things do you prefer to do?

R = Recognize Responsibilities. We have talked about the phrase, "I am responsible" and it is key here. The sooner we recognize the fact that we have a major role in the responsibility for how things are going in our lives, the sooner we are able to own those responsibilities. Once we recognize the responsibilities we have, we can begin to blend them with our personal preferences. Sometimes, this blending process reveals how much conflict there is between what we would really rather do and what we really *should* do. We need to be honest with ourselves about our preferences and our responsibilities if we are ever going to be able to figure this out. I can tell you that one conclusion I've drawn from both personal experience and observations from counseling others is that when we do the things we ought to do, there is a sense of fulfillment and self-worth that comes which always outweighs the momentary gratification of personal preference. So although I may prefer to play golf rather than exercise, I know that in the long run, the improvement to my health will bring greater value to my life.

Exercise: *What are your preferences? What are your responsibilities?*

DAY EIGHTY
PRIORITIES #2

I = Initiate Integration. The next step is to integrate our personal preferences with our responsibilities. There is sure to be conflict here. I believe this struggle has been going on since the dawn of time. For me, in keeping with the example of improving my health, I know I should be getting on a machine to workout. And yet I could justify doing what I really prefer to do—playing golf—because it also is exercise. But it is not the same. So in the midst of this conflict of thoughts, here's what I've discovered. I found that if I don't exercise first thing in the morning it does not get done that day because I will not do it later in the day. My preference may be to go play golf first thing, but what I should do is exercise. Here is where I need to integrate my preferences and my responsibilities. Again, this takes being honest with myself, and it takes some forethought and planning. My solution may be something like: I can only play golf if I have done my workout. Further, knowing that my workout only gets done if I do it first thing in the morning, I then commit to working out as soon as I get up.

O = Organize the Options. We've established that there will be conflicts between our preferences and our responsibilities. What I've found is that it is possible to organize our preferences and our responsibilities so that we can do both, because merely fulfilling our responsibilities without also doing what we like to do is not going to bring much joy into our lives. As we begin to look at where the conflicts are between our preferences and our responsibilities, we need to come up with some options.

Years ago when I began my adventure in physical conditioning, I was living in Michigan. I knew that I needed to exercise for at least 45 minutes, 5 days a week. I also knew that my strong preference was not to be outside when it was 20 degrees below zero. My preference to stay warm superseded my responsibility to be healthy. I had to come up with an option, and so that option was to purchase a treadmill. So, when we recognize conflicts, we can draw upon our creative powers to develop options that make both preference and responsibility possible.

R = Review the Resources. As we create options that allow us to do both our preference and our responsibility, there are multiple resources that can help make those options possible. When I was getting in shape, one of the resources I had was the money to buy equipment I could use indoors. Another resource was people who encouraged me on my journey. Receiving that encouragement was a preference that made the responsibility more palatable. As you evaluate yourself and your priorities, be thinking about all the things, places, and people that may be able to help you.

Exercise: *What options can you see that will begin to integrate your preferences with your responsibilities? What resources do you have to help you?*

DAY EIGHTY-ONE
PRIORITIES #3

PRIORITIES
P = Personalize Preferences
R = Recognize Responsibilities
I = Initiate Integration
O = Organize the Options
R = Review the Resources
I = Imagine and Inculcate the Ideal
T = Test the Template
I = Investigate Impediments
E = Establish Excellence
S = Stretch Towards Significance

I = Imagine and Inculcate the Ideal. Inculcate means to implant by repetition. This goes back to the strategy of daily, deliberate focus on the things that we are working towards. The ideal outcome of the integration of our responsibility and our personal preferences will be options that allow us to blend them in such a way as to love the process of doing what we really ought to do. As we imagine the ideal outcome, we begin to keep picturing that process again and again. Each day by affirmation, we continue to implant inside our thinking, inside our emotions, this captivating desire to do what we really are supposed to do, what we are designed to do, what our purpose in life is all about … and to love every moment of it.

T = Test the Template. This part is pretty simple. It's time to take what we've figured out about our priorities and put it into action. Let's make our schedule according to the priorities we've determined and see how it goes. Does it work? For me, the scheduling template that says "exercise later in the day" doesn't work. The one that says "exercise first thing in the morning" does work. Sometimes we can test the template by theory, but oftentimes we will need a test run to determine if it really works.

I = Investigate Impediments. There are going to be obstacles, challenges, and problems with the templates that we create. When we encounter them, we need to begin to find solutions. In the case of my health pursuits, there are days when I am busy from early in the morning until late at night. This means that there may be days when I don't get to exercise. I must find a solution to this impediment. It is amazing how creative we can become when we combine the joy of doing what we really want to do with the self-fulfillment of doing what we know we should do. If you find it difficult to come up with solutions, remember that your focus should be on the long range, big picture view of life, rather than the short-range difficulty. Solutions will come as you learn to look for them.

E = Establish Excellence. Since excellence is our goal in life, now we begin to create a rhythm of life based on the priorities we have established. At this point we've developed a plan and written it down. Now it's time to begin to thrive in the rhythm of excellence!

S = Stretch Towards Significance. As we find a rhythm of life and become excellent at embracing our priorities, we will find that our lives reach a place of significance. We all have the same number of hours in the day. Our path to significance can be found through determining our priorities and using that knowledge to schedule our calendars and make decisions.

I hope these few days have given you a starting place to begin to think about priorities in your life. Remember, this is a topic that should be reevaluated periodically. There may be seasons in life where some priorities shift, or where a lower priority (like work) might need a greater degree of time and focus than a higher priority. Your framework can be fluid, but I believe that it must be built in order for you to become the very best version of yourself.

Exercise: What is your ideal picture of your life with healthy priorities? How can you spend time visualizing this each day?

DAY EIGHTY-TWO |
LOYALTY |

Are you a loyal person? Think about it for a few moments. There are some people that are just loyal people. I don't know if this is something they are born with or if it is learned from the environment they are raised in. This brings another question: What does being a loyal person look like?

Loyalty is when we show support, allegiance, or faithfulness to a person, a value, or an organization. There is a spectrum of loyalty. On one end are the people who turn against the person or organization as soon as the wind changes direction. On the other end of the spectrum are the people who are blindly loyal, no matter what. This means that they remain committed without ever asking if what they are doing is moral or ethical or something they actually want to be committed to. I think most of us would like to be somewhere in between.

A great example of loyalty can be found in the military. Here, each soldier is loyal to the other and they are all loyal to the country they defend. This is a deep loyalty, one in which they will give up their life to protect their fellow soldier and their country. Their priorities are structured so that their loyalty is first and foremost to their country.

If you've done some reflecting and aren't sure you are a person of great loyalty, you may be wondering how you can improve that. The answer is that you have to be willing to sacrifice. The place where your loyalty lies must supersede the other priorities in your life, and that will always come with a cost. The question is: is that cost the right price to pay? Once you have determined if your loyalty is well placed, it is much easier to pay the price for that loyalty.

If you've found that you are a person of deep loyalty, that's wonderful. Loyalty is a beautiful quality in a person. However, you need to be aware of this trait being abused by others. Some people will discover how loyal you are and they will take advantage of your help simply because they know you will give it. This isn't healthy, and boundaries become crucial. If you know what your priorities are, it will make it easier to say no. It will also help you establish boundaries.

I want to be a person of well-placed loyalty. I want to be someone who can be counted on by those I am loyal to. I invite you to join me in this journey to being loyal – not blind-loyal, not fickle-loyal, but fierce-loyal.

Exercise: *List some people, values, or organizations in your life that you are loyal to. Would you describe that loyalty as fickle, blind, or fierce?*

DAY EIGHTY-THREE
LEAD BY EXAMPLE

The topic of modeling or exampling is a subject area that is often requested when I go to speak, and it is one that is on Susan's short list of books she would like me to write. This topic is particularly applicable if you are a parent and is also valuable when leading or training others. Really, any place in life that you want to have influence or that you are responsible to have influence, the idea of leading by example is key.

Let's think about it from a parenting perspective. As parents, we want so many things for our children, and there are also often things we *don't* want for them. I want my kids to be kind, respectful, hard-working. I don't want my kids to be lazy or entitled or selfish. Right? I find that most parents, including myself, don't want their kids to struggle with the same things that they themselves have struggled with. As an example, let's take cigarette smoking. Many parents smoke, but they don't like that they do it, they struggle with quitting, and they desperately don't want their children to smoke.

It's been my experience as well as my conclusion from a great deal of study that what we model, what we example to our children, is what they do. How our children relate to the world is very much based on how they view *us* relating to the world. We are the primary teachers and our actions and behaviors have far greater impact than our words.

I recognize this is not an easy thing. And the thought, "do as I say, not as I do", seems much easier. It just doesn't work.

The same goes for any sort of leadership relationship. Although it might be possible for a manager to get his team of people to work while he wastes most of his day on Facebook, the fact is that his team will never be highly effective. They will never be inspired to give their best or work their hardest when they know their leader is cutting corners on his own duties. And believe me … *they know.*

So what steps can we take to make this work *for* us? We decide what habits we want our kids or our teams to have, and then we begin to demonstrate those things to them. If we want our children to have integrity, we ourselves must be people of integrity. If we want our colleagues to be encouragers, then we ourselves must encourage. Now, this isn't just an "act" for when they are watching. These habits and characteristics must truly become a part of us if we hope to pass them on.

And in that process, we get to help others become the best versions of themselves *while also* working to become the best versions of ourselves. A win/win, if you ask me!

Exercise: *What is one trait that you are modeling to your kids or someone in your life that you need to change? What is one trait that you would like to begin practicing instead?*

DAY EIGHTY-FOUR
OBSERVATION

At Circle A, the leadership team invests a great deal of time in creating and maintaining an atmosphere. One of the key ways we do that is through observing what is going on in the lives of the young people there with us. During our staff training week, we go over some practices that help the leadership team be better at observation.

The skill of observation is one that will be of value to us in many different areas of life, not just as summer camp counselors. As employees, as leaders, as parents, as bosses, as humans … a keen sense of observation will be an asset to us in many facets of our journey. Even in the process of self-awareness, we need to develop the ability to observe things that are going on inside us and around us so that we can work towards enhancing the good things and correcting the not-so-good things.

When we are actively observing, our aim is to observe as much as possible, not just the point of focus in whatever is happening. Imagine we are watching a basketball game. We are usually focused on the ball and the action going on right there. If we widen our scope, how much more do we see? Players on the other side of the court are setting up a play and the defensive players are responding. Coaches are shouting instructions from the bench. Perhaps a player that left the game injured is about to come back in. A lot more is going on than just what is happening around the ball.

The same is true for our lives. Oftentimes when we are striving to achieve something, we are focused on it. This isn't a bad thing, in fact I've often taught on how to get laser-focused. What I'm addressing here is that there's a lot more going on that we should be aware of than just the point of focus. My experience has taught me that if we don't at least occasionally check what's going on in the periphery, it will impact what's happening at the point of focus.

Another important part of observation is learning *when* to look for certain things. There are cues that we can learn that will help set us up to observe what is most important. For example, when I first meet someone, my sense of observation is heightened. I observe words, tone of voice, body language, eye contact, degree of engagement, degree of distraction, etc. I know all of these things are important in any conversation, but particularly when I am meeting someone new. Recently I was in a large gathering, meeting many people for the first time. A friendly young man was standing just behind me in line. I said to him, "Do I need to stand on my head to know your name?" You see, he was wearing his name badge upside down.

He laughed and said, "You must be a very observant person. I have talked to over 50 people and you are the first one to even notice how I put my nametag upside down. I did it on purpose hoping it would start conversations."

Let's think about how we can expand our scope to see more of what is going on, and let's be deliberate about learning when to be especially observant. Let's observe ourselves as we pursue our goals, taking the time to look around every so often to see all the things that are going to impact our focus or our outcome.

Exercise: *What can you be deliberate about observing today?*

DAY EIGHTY-FIVE
THE COMFORT ZONE

#1: **INTRODUCTION**

In the process of becoming all we are created to be, it is important to invest some time in self-reflection. We must, in fact, get to know ourselves a little better. We must discover our strengths and talents and gifts so that we know where to focus our efforts towards growth.

As part of this self-assessment, we must also come to recognize a place in our lives known as "the comfort zone". If you've devoted any time at all to reading books in the self-help genre, you've no doubt run into this this phrase before. It's a common way to refer to the habits, thought patterns, social circles, and behavioral norms that we are comfortable living with. Discovering what our comfort zone is can be very beneficial in the process of becoming the best version of ourselves. Here's a quote that I have come to embrace about it: "Everything you want in life lies just outside your comfort zone."[15]

Now that can be a rather irritating statement, can't it? We cannot ignore the merit of learning to be grateful for what we have. Why shouldn't we just be thankful for the things that already exist in our zone of comfort, rather than wanting things that are outside of it?

Well, yes, there is plenty to be grateful for right inside our comfort zones. Of course there is, and we should practice gratitude daily. But, if we are going to live deliberately in the process of becoming all that we are created to be, we need to recognize that the process of change is not going to be comfortable. The fact is that the things we want to have or achieve or become will never be inside our comfort zone ... because if they were in our comfort zone, *we would already have them.*

The goal is to *expand* the comfort zone to include more and more of the things, attitudes, experiences, and significance that we truly want in life.

We are going to invest several days thinking about our comfort zone, and asking some questions that will help us find the courage and the energy to enlarge that comfort zone. Where does our comfort zone come from? What do we do when we are stuck in a comfort zone created by a social group or work environment? How do we move beyond our comfort zone? When we discover the answers to these questions, we are far better equipped to walk farther down the path of becoming the best versions of ourselves.

Exercise: *In what area of your life can you clearly see that your comfort zone is holding you back from something that you really want?*

DAY EIGHTY-SIX
THE COMFORT ZONE

#2: WHERE DOES IT **COME** FROM?

What is the comfort zone, really? How is it formed? I believe that it is something that morphs and changes over time, depending on a variety of factors: what we invest our time doing, who we invest our time with, how much we push ourselves, etc. However, the deepest parts of our comfort zone are actually built around our own self-image. If you believe yourself to be a certain way—physically unfit, or socially awkward, or slow with numbers—then your comfort zone will be built around activities and people and thought patterns that do not force you to interact with those perceived weaknesses.

Here's an example from one of our former leadership team members at Circle A. We were talking about food one day, and he related to me that if it weren't for having been through the program at Circle A as a camper, his diet would be very different. When he was younger, he stopped eating most vegetables and other nourishing foods. His mother had to go to great lengths to get him proper nutrition. Then, he started coming to Circle A and began to try foods. Each year he grew a little braver, tried a few new things, and began expanding his palate. One year as an LT he challenged himself to try one of his most dreaded foods: eggs. Prior to this, just the smell of eggs would cause him to gag. Well, he tried them and now EGGS are one of his favorite foods! He also told me that this created in him a love of trying new foods, which gave him a point of connection with his future wife.

If we look at this illustration, the comfort zone was in place because he believed that he only liked *certain* foods and anything outside of those foods would make him ill. His family sustained the zone by making sure that his meals included these foods. As he got older, he kept it up on his own by avoiding meals that he wasn't used to or comfortable with. Finally he stepped outside the zone and while not every experience has been a good one, there are far more enjoyable experiences that have expanded his comfort zone to include a much wider variety of foods.

Think about yourself. There are many things you believe to be true about yourself, and your comfort zone exists so that you do not have to challenge these beliefs. But what could your life look like if you do decide to challenge these beliefs? What joys and pleasures and victories and achievements might you be missing out on simply because you have allowed yourself to build a comfort zone that excludes them?

Exercise: What is one thing that you really want in life but feel incapable of achieving? Think about how your comfort zone might be distorting your perspective or hindering you from moving towards your goal?

DAY EIGHTY-SEVEN
THE COMFORT ZONE

#3: A **SHIELDED** SAFETY

I really enjoy *Star Trek*, and I have taken the time to watch it over the years. In the show, whenever a confrontation between two starships happens, the captains are given updates about the "shields" and how they are holding. The more recent technologies of *Star Trek* shields work as a force field around the ship, a bubble to protect the ship and its crew from external dangers. Some shields even have a cloaking capability, which renders the ship invisible to any outside forces. It occurs to me that our comfort zones work pretty much the same way: they exist to protect us from dangers that we perceive are coming near. A difference here is that the shields on *Star Trek* can be lowered pretty easily; the same cannot be said of the comfort zone.

The idea of lowering our shields when we feel faced with a threat is certainly counter-intuitive to our human nature. We know that we are safe in our comfort zone, and if safety is our primary purpose in life, then our shields should indeed remain perpetually raised.

I believe, however, if you are still committed to the process of reading this book, you are already convinced that your primary purpose in life is not safety.

And so, friends, we must be brave. We must lower our shields, and we must welcome the trials and challenges and growth opportunities that are sure to come our way. In Star Trek, the shields prevent anyone from transporting on or off the ship. If anyone wants to leave or come aboard, the shields must be down. Think of that analogy for a moment. Do you want to spend your whole life aboard a star ship? Or are there perhaps other worlds to explore? Are there perhaps other people who will make your life meaningful … people that one day you will want to bring aboard with you? *You'll never know if your shields are up.*

How do we lower our shields and move outside the comfort zone? It begins with a deliberate choice. We take small steps of exploration and bravery, and what we usually find is that we are far stronger than we ever gave ourselves credit for. Enough successful experiences erode our fears and make us bolder. We discover that our fear dissipates in the excited anticipation of the unknown challenge and adventure that lies on the path to becoming all that we are created to be.

Exercise: *Visualize your comfort zone as a shield around you, and then imagine lowering it. What is the first step of exploration that you are most drawn to take?*

DAY EIGHTY-EIGHT
THE COMFORT ZONE

#4: **GROUP** DYNAMICS

One place where we can get stuck in a comfort zone is when it is fueled by a social dynamic. Families, friends, work environments – they can all play a part in locking us into a limiting comfort zone.

Well-meaning family members or friends can affirm the self-concept that we have, and thereby help us construct and reinforce our comfort zone. For example, if mom believes that little Johnny just isn't good at music, she might shelter him from any experience where he would have the opportunity to make a fool of himself. She might disallow talent shows, she might say no to music lessons, she might purposefully arrange a family vacation so that he misses the homecoming dance. She might think she is doing him a favor with these actions, but it is building up a shield that he might never be able to lower.

It can go a step further when your circle of friends or family members or co-workers has the same comfort zone as you. If you have a circle of friends who all hate to exercise and seldom make good eating choices, then chances are you could be pulled into that same comfort zone. It might be easy and funny to mock the people who choose to make their health a higher priority, but it's going to lock you into a dangerous comfort zone that is validated by people who are already stuck in the same place. This type of social pressure to remain unchanged for the sake of the comfort of your peers can be a huge deterrent on the path to becoming all that you are created to be.

We should also recognize that sometimes the culture at our place of employment might add another obstacle. Sometimes a culture based on comparison and competition will aid coworkers who will deter you from going for a goal and leaving the comfort zone. There are any number of reasons they might do this. One could be that you are a part of their comfort zone. If you step out, they will have to change, they will have to adapt or even compete with you. The group dynamic of comfort zones tends to leave people all wanting to maintain a status-quo environment together, and this will never lead to any great success or significance in the work place.

One young woman shared a real-life experience with me about this. She was a hard worker and determined to pursue excellence in her job. Her boss continued to pile more and more assignments on her desk. She continued to accomplish each one. Her boss said to her one day, "What is it going to take to break you? The people of this office do not like the fact that you continue to do everything you are asked to do. They feel it makes them look bad. You need to adjust to the norm of your co-workers." *Unbelievable!* And yet this is the reality in a lot of work environments.

If you are in these situations—a social group that guards you from leaving a comfort zone or one that asks you to stay in their comfort zone—I would encourage you to think about how you can walk away from the limiting power of that group. It might mean that you have to leave completely … or it might mean that you just have to refuse to give that social group the permission to define your comfort zone by their own.

Exercise: *What is one social or family group that is defining part of your comfort zone? What steps can you take to break free of that in a healthy way?*

DAY EIGHTY-NINE
PARAMETERS

What is the boundary line for your dream?

It doesn't cost any more to dream big than it does to dream small. However, the reality is that most people dream small rather than dreaming big. Somehow, we often believe that a small dream won't seem so impossible, won't invite so much ridicule, and won't bring with it as much agony of defeat if it never becomes a reality.

The limiting factors that we place upon ourselves and the size of our dreams indicate a lack of belief in our ability to accomplish great things. So, for today, we are going to emphasize dreaming big. If you had *all* the talent and *all* the ability and *all* the resources and *all* the time and *all* the people you needed to accomplish *anything*, what then would be your goal for this year?

You see, when we begin to take off the limiting parameters within which most of us operate and begin to think in terms of the largeness of the possibilities of life, we have a whole different picture to look at.

What if we begin to look beyond where we ordinarily look?

Tear down the boundaries of fear. In this exercise, I am encouraging you to develop the wildest, biggest, most wonderful kind of a picture that you can generate. Think BIG. See the end - the most inspiring, exciting end you can imagine - from the beginning. In that process of big thinking, you will discover that there are boundaries that will fade away and perceived limitations that will be exposed as unnecessary parameters.

I am seeking to persuade you to get into that mode of thinking and begin to feel the freedom that it brings. When that takes place, there will be some great things, not only established as your goals, but also accomplished in your life.

Exercise: *If limitations were not a factor, what you would most like to accomplish?*

DAY NINETY
IT TAKES A LIFETIME

I don't know how you feel about it, but it seems to me that growth ought to take place far more rapidly and obviously than what it sometimes does. We live in a society that desires—and frequently demands—immediacy. If something takes more than 4 steps and 4 minutes, many are not interested or willing to commit to the process at all.

The fact is, however, that personal growth tends to take a long time. It comes a little bit at a time over a long period of committed focus on it. If learning and implementing the concepts of goal-setting, proper self-image, positive attitude, and excellence were a short and simple process, there wouldn't be countless thousands of books written on the subjects. There would be one simple book, with a simple process, and everyone who followed that process would suddenly be proficient at all those things. Boy, I wish it could work that way! Don't you?

But that's not the way it works. Here's what I've discovered about it: *personal growth is far more about the deliberate process of engaging each day than it will ever be about a final result.*

What do I mean by that? Simply this: you and I can learn all of these principles—we can memorize the definitions and quote the experts and even make significant strides in our own lives to example the best of ourselves—but on any given day, for a wide variety of reasons, we can find it easy to forget it all.

If we do not continually engage on a daily basis with the type of thinking and reading and socializing and dreaming and purposeful decision-making that leads us towards personal growth, we will deteriorate faster than we even know what happened to us.

It is not enough to know these principles. Our task is not merely to learn material … our task is to choose daily to participate in our own growth.

And that, my friends, takes a lifetime.

So … we must be patient. We must recognize that our becoming is about the journey. Most importantly, we must remember that if we fall away or forget to participate in our own growth, we can always come back. Every day is a new day and we have a lifetime to work on it.

Exercise: Think of one area of personal growth in your life where you feel like you should have "arrived" by now. Reevaluate that belief in the context of what we learned today. What is one choice you can make today in that area?

CONCLUSION

As this book comes to a close, I think it's important to remind ourselves that there is only one thing that would keep you or me from taking what we have studied in these pages and making some major, positive change in our lives.

Ourselves.

I am the only one who can get in my way and derail progress and change. I am the only one who holds the responsibility to continue the positive habits that I have formed for the *next* 90 days and beyond. And you are the only one who can do it for you.

Sometimes I imagine that I can just decide it for you. I can't, of course, but if I could I would just flip a switch in your brain that would keep you committed to a path of positive change in your life. If I could, I would remind you daily of all the lessons you have discovered in these pages, of all the ways you have determined to take steps towards becoming all that you are created to be. Unfortunately, I am not empowered to do that for you. The good news? *You are and you can.*

Now it doesn't mean that everything will go perfectly. It doesn't mean that there will be no moments of disappointment and no moments of failure and no moments of falling short of the mark. In fact, I can almost guarantee you that all of those things will happen in the next 90 days and beyond. We know from our experiences that the challenges of life will come. The question we have before us is what we will do with those things. Will they become our excuses to hold ourselves back? Or will we use all those things, combined with what we've learned in this little book, and continually make progress towards something better? Maybe what we need to do is start back at day one and complete another 90 days.

Only you can get in your way. Only you can hold yourself back. Only you can derail your path of personal growth. Because every external circumstance and opinion and discouragement will affect you only in the way that you allow it to. Stepping stone or stumbling block … is it your choice.

In the same way, only you can take the information and the experiences of yesterday and put those together in such a way as to propel yourself forward today. It is up to *you*, it is up to *me*. I must encourage myself every day. Not in a proud or haughty or arrogant sort of way, but in a way that recognizes that I am worth the effort of moving towards excellence and purpose and fulfillment. Not only am I worth it, but I am also capable of it. Not only am I capable of it, but I am also created for it. I am created for it and when I become what I am created to be, I inspire and encourage others to do that very same thing.

And so do you.

Exercise: Write down some encouragement for yourself today. Write down some reasons why you are worth the effort. Write down some people that you will influence by your example.

CIRCLE A RANCH AND THRIVE

A NOTE ABOUT **CIRCLE A RANCH**

After reading this book, you may be interested to find out more information about our Circle A Ranch program. We currently operate Circle A Camp programs each summer in various places around the United States. We hope to soon expand these locations internationally as well.

For more information about Circle A Ranch, please visit

www.circleacamp.com

We have also just completed a modernization and overhaul of the original *Dynamic Living* material into a new study series called *THRIVE*.

For more information on materials, 2-Day events, seminars, and facilitator support, visit

www.thrivestudy.com

WORKS **CITED**

Day 7

1. Maxwell, John C., and Jim Dornan. *Becoming a Person of Influence: How to Positively Impact the Lives of Others*. Nashville, Tenn.: T. Nelson, 1997. 129. Print. Quoting speechwriter Robert Orben.

Day 15

2. "Count Your Blessings." Lyrics. Web. 3 Oct. 2015.

Day 16

3. Grant, Dave. *The Ultimate Power*. Old Tappan, N.J.: F.H. Revell, 1983. 19. Print.

Day 26

4. "Why We Procrastinate." *Psychology Today*. 1 July 2005. Web. 20 Sept. 2015.

Day 27

5. *The Principia: Mathematical Principles of Natural Philosophy* (1687), 3rd edition (1726), trans. I. Bernard Cohen and Anne Whitman (1999), Axioms, or Laws of Motion, Law 1, 416. Print.

6. "Why We Procrastinate." *Psychology Today*. 1 July 2005. Web. 20 Sept. 2015.

Day 28

7. "Why We Procrastinate." *Psychology Today*. 1 July 2005. Web. 20 Sept. 2015.

Day 32

8. Maxwell, John C. "Leadership Wired Blog." *The John Maxwell Company*. 6 May 2014. Web. 1 Oct. 2015. http://www.johnmaxwell.com/blog/delegation-by-way-of-development.

Day 67

9. Matthew 12:34

Day 73

10. Tolkien, J. R. R. "Chapter 4: A Short Cut to Mushrooms." *The Fellowship of the Ring: Being the First Part of The Lord of the Rings*. 2nd ed. Boston: Houghton Mifflin, 2001. 97. Print.

Day 77

11. "Quote Investigator." *Quote Investigator*. Web. 5 Oct. 2015. http://quoteinvestigator.com/2011/03/30/not-inferior/.

Day 78

12. Lucado, Max. "Chapter 5: Maxims." *When God Whispers Your Name*. Nashville: Word Pub., 1999. 44. Print.

Day 78

13. Thoreau, Henry David. *Walden, Or, Life in the Woods*. New York: Modern Library, 1950. 13. Print.

Day 79

14. *A Few Good Men*. Dir. Rob Reiner. 1992. Film.

Day 85

15. Hansen, Mark Victor, and Robert G. Allen. *The One Minute Millionaire: The Enlightened Way to Wealth*. New York: Three Rivers, 2009. Print.

BIOS

SKIP ROSS

Skip Ross is the owner, founder, and director of Circle A Ranch. He and his wife Susan have dedicated their lives to making a difference through this ministry, and have spent the last 37 years giving their summers to the work of Circle A. Skip is the author of several books and is best known for the *Dynamic Living Seminar*. He has traveled the globe teaching the principles of attitude development and leadership to millions of people for over 50 years. He is a successful business executive, recording artist, and motivational speaker. He is founder and president of the OFIDA Project, a Crown IBO with Amway, and a graduate of Westmont College and Fuller Theological Seminary.

MELODY FARRELL

Melody Farrell co-owns and operates a production company, Echo Media Group, and a publishing company, Lost Poet Press. She is associate director of Circle A Ranch and has held numerous leadership positions in various churches and ministries throughout her life. She, along with her husband Chris, was on the founding launch team of Element Church in Tampa, Florida, and currently serves as their Administrative Pastor. She holds a degree from Lee University and she operates a successful Amway business. She is a podcaster, a vocalist, and a mother of two. Skip is Melody's father, and she is honored to join him on this project.

MIKE COOKE

Mike Cooke grew up in New Jersey and began attending Circle A at age eleven. He invested every summer at Circle A for many years as a camper, auxiliary stuff, and Leadership Team member, and went on to become a deeply valued and influential part of the ongoing ministry of Circle A. Mike graduated from Rensselaer Polytechnic Institute with a Bachelor of Science degree. He resides in Florida with his wife, Maria and their son, James. He serves as a house church leader at his local church as well as a teacher for the children's ministry. He remains committed to the future of Circle A and *Dynamic Living*!